Praise for
The Bully-Proof Workplace

"Very rarely do I find a book that is eminently readable and incredibly practical and works to solve a complex problem. *The Bully-Proof Workplace* achieves that trifecta. The stories outlined here could be in any of our workplace environments, yet Dean and Shepard come up with usable strategies that are universal in their impact. Leaders are increasingly judged based on their ability to handle the people under their tutelage, and though much has been written about leadership and followership, the scourge of bullying in the workplace has been significantly underanalyzed. No more. This book should be on every manager's bookshelf and should be shared throughout the workplace. If that happens, bullying in the workplace may become a historical footnote."

—STEPHEN K. KLASKO, MD, MBA,
president and CEO of Thomas Jefferson University
and Jefferson Health

"Workplace bullying has been swept under the rug, probably as a result of the lack of strategies for dealing with the bully. Learn how to recognize the type of bully, plan on how to confront him or her, and then execute the plan. All of that is in this invaluable book."

—MADELINE BELL,
president and CEO of Children's Hospital of Philadelphia

"*The Bully-Proof Workplace* provides a combination of research-based context, encouragement, and diagnostic and therapeutic tools to those grappling with bullying in their workplace. Everyone working in a group, whether or not in management, will find this guidebook thought-provoking. This is a text to read and then keep within arm's reach for reference should a bully emerge in your workplace."

—William J. T. Strahan,
EVP of HR at Comcast Cable

"In today's workplace, organizations have a responsibility to create an environment that enables the best in every employee. Simply put, bullies and bullying behavior cost companies millions of dollars, not to mention the psychological and emotional toll they inflict on people. *The Bully-Proof Workplace* offers an important and useful framework for understanding bullies and addressing bullying behavior, as well as providing practical and applicable strategies for dealing with them. Bravo!"

—Caroline F. McCabe, PsyD,
director of Executive Talent,
Leadership & Team Intelligence at Cisco

"*The Bully-Proof Workplace* gives us the tools to root out destructive behaviors in our work environment. As we see increases in bullying across the nation, it is critical to identify those behaviors and to learn how to create a corporate culture where all employees can thrive. This book couldn't be more timely. Kudos!"

—Theresa Bryce Bazemore,
president of Radian Guaranty Inc.

"As chair of a global law firm, I feel it is imperative that our lawyers understand the issue of bullying from a personal perspective as a leader in the firm as well as its implication for our clients, especially as antibullying legislation increases in this country. *The Bully-Proof Workplace* is a book for understanding the phenomenon of bullying and how to deal with it and thus create a productive workplace. The recommended tactics and strategies for reducing bullying will allow strategic thinking, learning, and leading to flourish."

—JAMI WINTZ MCKEON,
chair of Morgan, Lewis & Bockius LLP

"As the leader of a global executive search firm and a practicing executive search consultant, I could not feel more strongly that we have a responsibility to weed out bullies during the assessment part of our placement protocol. *The Bully-Proof Workplace* provides a way to observe behavior to determine if a candidate is a potential bully as there is no place for bullies in the workplace."

—JUDITH VON SELDENECK,
founder, chairwoman, and CEO of Diversified Search

"It takes courage to stand up to a bully. It also takes know-how. Dean and Shepard show you how in *The Bully-Proof Workplace*. This practical guide, filled with case studies, checklists, and even scripts, will give you or the people you coach the tools they need to put a stop to workplace bullying.

—MARGARET H. GREENBERG,
executive coach and coauthor of *Profit from the Positive*

"If you think bullying happens only in schoolyards, think again. Workplace bullying is a tremendous problem, affecting 65 million people per year, especially women. If you are one of them, don't rely on the HR department to protect you. Read this book and learn how to protect yourself."

—ALBERT J. BERNSTEIN, PHD,
bestselling author of *Emotional Vampires*

"Most of us have dealt with impossible coworkers—but who ever thought of them as bullies? Or that workplaces can unnecessarily encourage them? Executive coaches Peter Dean and Molly Shepard are on to something important, quantifying bullies' burden on morale and efficiency and offering practical ways to reform or repel them."

—ANNE KREAMER,
author of *It's Always Personal*

THE
BULLY-PROOF
WORKPLACE

THE
BULLY-PROOF
WORKPLACE

ESSENTIAL **STRATEGIES**,
TIPS, AND **SCRIPTS** FOR
DEALING WITH THE
OFFICE SOCIOPATH

PETER J. DEAN MS, PhD
AND
MOLLY D. SHEPARD MS, MSM

NEW YORK CHICAGO SAN FRANCISCO ATHENS
LONDON MADRID MEXICO CITY MILAN

1 2 3 4 5 6 7 8 9   LCR   22 21 20 19 18 17

ISBN 978-1-259-85966-3
MHID   1-259-85966-5

e-ISBN 978-1-259-85965-6
e-MHID   1-259-85965-7

Design by Lee Fukui and Mauna Eichner

McGraw-Hill Education books are available at special quantity discounts to use as premiums and sales promotions or for use in corporate training programs. To contact a representative, please visit the Contact Us pages at www .mhproffessional.com.

*To our friends and colleagues who believe that a
productive workplace is a civil and respectful workplace.
They stand up to bullies every day, and they protect and defend
others from the consequences of the bullies' bad behavior.
Their kindness, courage, and vigilance will serve to end
bullying behavior in the workplace and our society.*

CONTENTS

ACKNOWLEDGMENTS

We wish to acknowledge our appreciation of our one-of-a-kind book agent and initial editor, Jane von Mehren of Aevitas Creative Management. Jane helped us clarify what this book could be. She masterfully empowered us to optimize the writing process.

The project was acquired by a gifted senior editor at McGraw-Hill, Casey Ebro, who provided another round of high-level editing and editorial clarity. Sincere thanks to Mauna Eichner and Lee Fukui.

We also want to thank Nan Myers for her backup proofreading and editing and Monica Warner Dimpfl, who supported yet again another book project with her usual patience and thoughtfulness.

In this book, we are speaking for the many clients from our collective experience who have shared their experiences of being harassed and bullied. Their stories are represented throughout the book, and we thank them for helping us appreciate the difficulties faced by those who are oppressed in the workplace.

Over the years, we have encountered very knowledgeable people from the arenas of psychology, management and leadership development, ethics, communications, and organizational design. Whether in person or in print, their insights have led to our enhanced learning.

PROLOGUE

Knowing what's right doesn't mean much
unless you do what's right.
—THEODORE ROOSEVELT

Our decision to write this book began with the nightly news. It was November 2013, and Keith Olbermann was breaking the Bullygate story about the National Football League (NFL) team the Miami Dolphins.[1] On an almost daily basis, Richie Incognito and two other fellow offensive linemen, John Jerry and Mike Pouncey, taunted Jonathan Martin, calling him names and using racist epithets as well as derogatory and homophobic language. They made jokes about slavery and obscene statements about his sister, and they touched him improperly.[2] The sociopathic bullying got so bad that Incognito even left threatening phone messages on Martin's phone:

> "Hey, what's up, you half [racial slur] piece of [expletive]?
> I saw you on Twitter. You have been training for 10 weeks.
> I want to [expletive] in your [expletive] mouth. I am going to slap your [expletive] mouth. I am going to slap your real mother across the face [laughter]. [Expletive] You, you're still a rookie. I'll kill you."

You'd think that Martin, a 6-foot-5-inch, 312-pound football player, would be bully-proof and not be intimidated by this behavior. But the reality was that he had no idea how to deal with Incognito and his pals. Ultimately, Martin abruptly left the team on October 28, 2013, and checked himself into a hospital to receive psychiatric counseling for significant emotional distress. As the controversy unfolded, Lydon Murtha, another Dolphins player, told Olbermann what many people think: playing football is a man's job, and if there is a weak link on the team, it has to be weeded out. It is the leader's job to take care of it. As Bullygate unfolded, the Miami Dolphins coaches at first denied knowing anything about the hazing or bullying. Eventually, though, Incognito was suspended, and the offensive line coach, Jim Turner, who allegedly had directed Incognito to "toughen Martin up," was let go.

As we watched the coverage of this bullying scandal, we were struck by the similarity between the lack of know-how in dealing with sociopathic bullying behavior in the locker room and the lack of know-how in dealing with it in the corporate world. Like many people who are bullied, Martin had no idea how to handle it. Nor did anyone else—from his teammates and his coaches to the front office. For the NFL, being tough and aggressive is part of the job. And for that reason some people were at first reluctant to label what Martin had suffered as bullying. But by the time the NFL and Ted Wells, the independent investigator, issued the report of the incident investigation in February 2014, sports commentators and the Miami Dolphins head coach, Joe Philbin, were discussing the case in terms of acceptable workplace behavior rather than questioning who said what. Coach Philbin agreed to cooperate fully with the NFL's inquiry into the hazing allegations and to accept its findings. In a few short months, many in the media and in the sports world had come to see that what happened to Jonathan Martin was, in fact, no different from the bullying incidents that we are called in as coaches to resolve again and again in "traditional" workplaces.

For most of us, the term *bullying* conjures up the schoolyard: the big kid who picks on the smaller one, often with a posse of hangers-on serving as witnesses and backup. In fact, schoolyard bullying remains rampant: in 2012 the David Mathews Center for Civic Life reported that every seven minutes a child is bullied on a school playground and 85 percent of those incidents happen without an adult's intervening. It also found that 100,000 children have carried guns to school as a result of being bullied. Yet many assume that kids outgrow bullying behavior and that adults can withstand encounters with a bully—but as Jonathan Martin's story shows, nothing could be further from the truth.

So what does it mean to be bullied by the office sociopath? According to the U.S. Department of Health and Human Services, bullying is defined by three elements:

1. There is an imbalance of power in which the bully uses his or her position to control or harm others.

2. The pattern of behavior is repeated and escalates over time.

3. The bully targets a person or group in a manner that is unwelcome by the targets.

From our experience as executive coaches, however, we don't believe this framework goes far enough. Sociopathic bullying exists in a wide variety of behaviors that intimidate and shut down the productivity of others. We have categorized bullies into four types: the Beliers, the Blockers, the Braggarts, and the Brutes. Each type uses different bullying tactics and is dealt with differently. In the chapters that follow, we will deconstruct them and offer solutions for dealing with each type.

We have written *The Bully-Proof Workplace* to share the antidotes we have developed over more than three decades in our executive coaching practice at The Leader's Edge/Leaders By Design. We offer proven strategies for ridding the workplace of sociopaths and the types of bullying they employ, whether you are the individual being targeted by a bully, a manager dealing with its effects on the team, or a CEO or senior leader who wants to change the culture of your organization.

We provide tools and strategies for handling the four types of bullies, scripts to use while confronting someone who has targeted you, and advice on how to enlist others to help you resolve this unhealthy situation. You will learn how to stand up to bullies, grow and develop at work, and not be forced to leave a job because of a bully.

A manager, director, or senior executive will gain the ability to identify bullying, deal with it swiftly, and introduce zero tolerance for such behavior in the workplace. Executives willing to use a policy statement and support appropriate tenets of behavior will have a blueprint for doing so. Additionally, if you are a manager and have bullying tendencies that sometimes creep into your own interactions, we have recommendations and tips on how to monitor yourself.

Readers at all levels will learn how to use active listening, how to engage with others respectfully to handle bullying situations, and how to create a productive culture in any workplace or organization. We spend 60 percent of our time at work. Having the majority of our lives negatively affected by bullying and functioning in a poor work culture are conditions no one should have to endure and no leader should have in his or her organization. With *The Bully-Proof Workplace*, you won't have to.

THE
BULLY-PROOF
WORKPLACE

BULLYING: A WORKPLACE CRISIS

If you are neutral in situations of injustice,
you have chosen the side of the oppressor.
—DESMOND TUTU

Sixty-five million workers in the United States are affected by workplace bullying each year. The numbers are staggering—and on the rise—both in the United States and globally. A study by Charlotte Rayner and her colleagues at the Manchester School of Management found that one in four people have been bullied at work.[1] Perhaps not surprisingly, women are more often the targets than men. In her book *The Need to Say No*, Jill Brooke reports that one-third more women than men are bullied.[2] Roughly one in four American workers have said that they've dealt with bullying at some point, according to a 2014 survey by the Workplace Bullying Institute (WBI).[3] And a study conducted by the National Institute for Occupational Safety and Health (NIOSH) found that

25 percent of the companies that participated reported some degree of bullying in the preceding year.[4] The 2014 WBI survey indicated that 72 percent of American workers are aware that workplace bullying happens, 21 percent have witnessed it, and 27 percent have suffered from abusive bullying at work.[5] The Society for Human Resource Management (SHRM) found 56 percent of U.S. employers do not have workplace bullying policies, although 35 percent of the U.S. workforce has reported being bullied at work.[6]

These statistics may surprise many, especially those who believe that bullying is a schoolyard phenomenon that we simply outgrow. We believe, however, that where bullying is concerned, there is a strong connection between schools and the workplace. Bullying behaviors exhibited by youths in schools eventually become habitual and move into the workplace. Bullying learned at work is showcased at home to children and thus makes its way back into schools. It is a vicious cycle. Teachers know that bullying exemplified in children's behavior at school is often a reflection of what their parents bring home from their work.

The reality is that in the workplace, bullying takes on numerous different forms. Although 56 percent of workplace bullying is top down, that is, a manager bullies a subordinate, more than 33 percent of bullying is between coworkers and 11 percent is bottom up. All too often this repeated behavior leads to the targets leaving the company—whether because, like Jonathan Martin described in the Prologue, they no longer can put up with the abuse or because their performance suffers and they are let go. Yet corporate employers are still in denial about bullying. According to the WBI (2014), more than 56 percent of employers deny it exists, discount its effects, or rationalize the behavior.[7]

The loss of talent alone can take an enormous financial toll on an organization because replacing a performer can cost two to three times that person's salary. More difficult to measure are the physical and mental health impairments caused by stress, as well as the social harm done within the organization when people have difficulty building meaningful and trusting relationships. What thrives in a workplace where bullying is tolerated is depression, anxiety, customer complaints, and litigation. The quality of work, productivity, employee loyalty, and engagement decline, and if the bullying is left unchecked, the bottom line of the organization is hurt. In our executive coaching practice, we have also seen that bullies sometimes select targets because of their proclivity to suggest ideas outside the normal boundaries of groupthink—that is, suggestions that may rock the boat or go against the opinions of the boss—which results in the loss of creativity and innovative thinking. In this chapter, we will define bullying and explore its impact in the workplace and its cost to businesses.

Andrea Adams was one of the first researchers to use the term *workplace bullying* in her book *Bullying at Work*, which is based on her study of the mistreatment of bank employees.[8] Her research showed that workplace bullying behavior includes a wide range of overt and covert behaviors of intimidation. The office sociopaths are insensitive to others, lack a social conscience, and are interested only in their personal needs and desires without concern about their behavior toward others. They seldom feel guilt, and they do not think there is anything wrong in their bullying others. They see everybody else as outside of themselves. They are liars, gossipers, hypocrites, controllers, and boasters, and they act without impulse control.

Indeed, through our own proprietary research and work as executive coaches, we have come to recognize bullying as an observable behavior that features several basic components. First, bullying is intentionally negative, aggressive, and malicious toward others who often have talent or expertise but who are otherwise less powerful than the bullies. Second, it is repeated persistently, usually in front of others, to wear down the targets. Bullying is not an occasional or infrequent expression of frustration. Rather, it is meant to harass, coerce, humiliate, demean, dominate, exclude, and/or subjugate other people. It purposely diminishes the targets' ability to work and redirects their energy toward being on the defense. Third, the bullies often close down avenues of communication, making it difficult for the targets to speak up for themselves. Most important, the effect of the bullying doesn't stop with the targets. It influences others in the workplace and can demotivate or instill fear, anxiety, stress, and a sense of powerlessness throughout the culture, which can, in turn, inhibit loyalty, creativity, and positive energy. Some who use bullying tactics do so believing that the culture supports it or, worse, that it is how to get ahead in the company.

Today, most employers tend to deny, discount, or rationalize bullying behavior—in because of a lack of understanding of the problem and how to deal with it. According to the Workplace Bullying Institute (WBI), some employers even encourage it. Only 16 percent of employers acknowledge it and condemn it, and just 12 percent of employers want to eliminate bullying in their organizations. If CEOs and executives do not acknowledge, condemn, and seek to eliminate bullying, employers give cover to office sociopaths as a result. The chart in Figure 1.1, reported in 2014 by the WBI, shows employers' responses to bullying in the workplace.

We know from experience that bullies and bully bosses stall, rather than speed up, productivity and engagement at work. They also impede the growth and development of talent in the company. In contrast, creating a zero-tolerance policy for bullying and encouraging managers to use their positive power and

What Are Employers Saying?

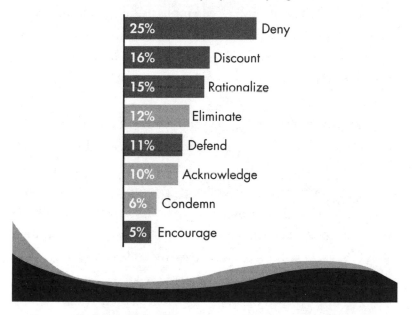

FIGURE 1.1 Employers' Responses to Bullying in the Workplace

Source: 2014 WBI U.S. Workplace Bullying Survey, February 2014, Gary Namie, PhD, research director, with assistance from Daniel Christensen and David Phillips.

influence to increase worker engagement leads to reenergized levels of productivity. An emotionally connected and interpersonally engaged workforce will be more innovative, creative, and productive—and that means higher profits.

BULLYING BEHAVIOR AT ALL LEVELS

In all sectors of the workplace, no level of employee or size of organization is immune from bullying. Numerous state governments have recognized this issue as well. In 2013 the Healthy Workplace Bill was introduced by the WBI in 24 states in an attempt to bring attention to this national issue and enact laws against workplace bullying. In light of an increased emphasis on human resources, emotional and social intelligence, policies that protect workers' rights, and the many companies that claim their people are their most important asset, it may seem surprising that bullying is so widespread today.

The growth of corporate power, the role of management, the stressors in the workplace, and a variety of historical factors have led to the increase of bullying in the workplace. Three outcomes of this increase in workplace bullying, according to the Society for Human Resource Management, have been decreased morale (68 percent of companies surveyed), increased stress and/or depression levels (48 percent of companies surveyed), and decreased trust and integrity among coworkers.

THE COSTS OF BULLYING

Ironic, isn't it, that the very managers who have been focusing on the bottom line to impress their corporate bosses have brought about an increase in bullying behavior that ultimately diminishes the very profits they are trying to increase? In a 2013 *Harvard Business Review* article, Porath and Pearson reported the results of a poll of 800 managers and employees in 17 industries that showed the effects of incivility on the job.[9] *Incivility* is not a soft term. It refers to a range of behaviors from minor acts of thoughtlessness and unchecked rudeness to acts of malice, which includes bullying behavior. The consequences for those employees on the receiving end of the full range of incivility that Porath and Pearson suggest include the following:

- 48 percent intentionally decreased their work effort.

- 47 percent intentionally decreased the time spent at work.

- 38 percent intentionally decreased the quality of their work.

- 80 percent lost work time worrying about a bullying incident.

- 63 percent lost work time avoiding a bully who had offended them.

- 66 percent said that their performance declined.

- 78 percent said that their commitment to the organization declined.

- 12 percent said that they left their job because of the uncivil treatment.

- 25 percent admitted to taking their frustration out on customers.

In 2011, Accountemps surveyed 150 executives and 1,000 senior managers from Fortune 1000 companies (the 1,000 largest American companies, ranked according to revenue) and asked them, "What percentage of your time is wasted resolving staff personality conflicts?"[10] These senior leaders said that they spent an average of 18 percent of their time on these issues. That translates into more than seven hours each week spent on resetting employee relationships, mending the consequences of incivility and bullying behavior, and getting work back on track.

Clearly, bullying is detrimental to workplace productivity, but it also can damage the bottom line. The potential dollar cost to American-based companies from bullying, according to Dr. Paul

Rosch, president of the American Institute of Stress (AIS), is $300 billion a year in terms of diminished productivity, employee turnover, and insurance.[11]

According to the Crisis Prevention Institute (CPI), "Research has clearly demonstrated that when targets [of bullying] believe someone at work has treated them disrespectfully, half will lose work time worrying about future interactions with the instigator, and half will contemplate changing jobs to avoid a recurrence."[12]

Research conducted by Know Bull: Anti-Bullying By Design showed that in Australia, the financial costs to business of workplace bullying is estimated at between A$6 and A$13 billion a year, which includes indirect costs such as absenteeism, labor turnover, loss of productivity, and legal expenses.[13] The average claim for stress from bullying is A$41,186, whereas the average claim for physical injury is A$23,441.

According to the United Kingdom–based Chartered Management Institute, every year 100 million days of productivity over the entire U.K. workforce are lost because of absenteeism caused by bullying.

Whether it is the insidious Belier making snide comments in a meeting that challenge another's credibility, the sarcastic Blocker who excludes people's contributions by shutting them down, the attention-seeking Braggart who shows blatant disregard for others' time by talking too much, or the anger-filled Brute yelling, threatening, and pounding his fist on the table, all bullies generate a negative and toxic work environment that results in increases in hypertension, panic attacks, and depression among employees. Both the targeted workers and other staff members may leave an organization because of a bullying culture, resulting in losses of talent and intellectual capital, not to mention losses in productivity when new employees need to be brought up to speed. In 2014, the WBI reported that for each worker bullied out of her job who earned a $50,000 salary, the recruiting and replacement expenses were at least $75,000. There were also potential litigation fees if a bullied employee sued for damages.[14] The WBI has reported that each threat of a lawsuit costs a company $30,000, and if a case goes to court, it will cost at least $60,000 before it even goes to trial.

The increases in healthcare and legal expenditures and decreases in productivity, along with the fact that replacing a worker can cost two or three times that person's salary to develop the same level of talent to replace him or her, add an enormous financial burden on a company. And if a company is dealing with all of these issues, it is also putting its good name and reputation at risk.

For the bullied person, the costs are more personal but no less devastating. The workplace becomes like a psychological prison of hesitation, mindless thinking, and negative expectations that drains energy and reduces overall productivity, making going to work a miserable daily experience. According to Dr. Gary Namie of the WBI and the founder of the Campaign Against Workplace Bullying, some people become less trusting of their colleagues after being bullied. In addition, he has reported that 82 percent of people targeted by a bully leave their workplace—38 percent leave for health reasons, and 44 percent after receiving unwarranted negative performance appraisals.

WORKPLACE BULLIES IN THE PAST

I would rather be a little nobody, than to be an evil somebody.
—ABRAHAM LINCOLN

Although bullies have existed since the beginning of time, their numbers began increasing in U.S. workplaces when layers of management were introduced at the start of the era of mass production.

Soon after the Civil War, the growth of corporate America as we know it began. As the robber barons—Cornelius Vanderbilt, John Pierpont ("J. P.") Morgan, John D. Rockefeller, and Andrew Carnegie among them—expanded their control over various industries by acquiring more and more companies, their organizations became so large that they were no longer able to oversee them on their own. They began hiring managers to help get the work done, and management was charged with overseeing workers.

This period, as Ralph Estes points out in *Tyranny of the Bottom Line*, saw companies evolve into many divisions, territories, and subsidiaries, making them look more like empires.[15] As owners replaced themselves with non-owning managers, the managers promised greater efficiency and increased profits, which they "guaranteed" with their professional credentials. Owners were no longer interested in whether their companies were fulfilling their chartered purpose. Instead, they wanted only profits reports. Over time, the profits reports (whether to shareholders or to single owners) became the *only* performance report. This sole focus on profits led to an accumulation of power in the management ranks as less and less attention was paid to the relationship between managers and workers lest it have a negative impact on profits.

At the turn of the twentieth century, Frederick W. Taylor emerged as an important force in American business. Although his system of scientific management was designed to help managers improve efficiency at work as well as to promote practices that were good for the managers *and* the employees, corporate managers understood it only as a way to get more work out of people. Taylor was striving for ways to continually increase the efficiency of any task by increasing the output of the worker. Little thought was given to the way in which the system viewed workers as cogs in the wheel whose rights or needs were ignored in favor of the overall efficiency of the company. Managers had the power of sanctions over hourly workers. They were in control, and they were charged with increasing profits. The result: bullying became commonplace as a means to force employees to work harder under the threat that they would lose their jobs.

The growth in the power of management led to more workplace bullying, a trend that continues to this day. In recent decades, globalization, technology, and the speed of change have led to an ever more competitive business landscape, which has created the kind of high-pressure work environment that brings about the four types of bullying.

Attempts to Balance the Relationship Between Managers and Workers

As early as the start of the twentieth century, there were some who recognized the imbalance of power between managers and workers. Even Frederick Winslow Taylor, in his classic *The Principles of Scientific Management*, suggested ways in which managers and workers could cooperate to solve workplace problems together.[16] In Taylor's view, both have a stake in cooperating: management controls the playing field by scheduling who does what work when, and workers control quality, quantity, and costs. Taylor also believed that if workers were demotivated, the blame lay with management, not the employees.

Frank and Lillian Gilbreth, both early adherents of Taylorism, broke from Taylor when it became obvious that Taylor found it unacceptable to consider the workers as people, rather than as mechanical cogs in a wheel. The Gilbreths wanted managers and workers to team together to produce quality goods quickly and efficiently, but they wanted the process of work to include what was going on in the minds of the people doing the work. They wanted managers to lead their teams by using what we now call "emotional and social intelligence," whereas Taylor favored "enforcement" by "efficiency experts" as the primary tool of management.

During the Depression, the exploitation of workers became common—when work was hard to come by, workers became more tolerant of bullying managers. John Steinbeck's Pulitzer Prize–winning novel *The Grapes of Wrath* is a brilliant portrait of those desperate times. In reality, though, there were few Tom Joads who would risk losing their jobs by speaking up about the terrible working conditions the rank and file endured.

Changes in the Work Culture

During World War II, a huge influx of women and minorities entered the workforce. Women shifted from working at home to lending a hand in heavy industry, filling in for the men who went to war. African-Americans flocked northward in greater numbers in hopes of industry jobs. After the war, women didn't all leave the workplace, having discovered the benefits of working, and minority workers wanted to maintain the higher wages they'd begun enjoying with factory jobs in the North.

In our research, many white men reported that it seemed as if women and minorities just showed up at work one day. In their minds, the fact that the men were there first was no small distinction. And many felt that every woman or minority kept a man out of the workforce who had already paid his dues—and that women and minorities had cut into the queue. Some men repressed their feelings of outrage, but others were vocal in their opposition and anger—often resulting in direct or indirect bullying. The 1979 film *Norma Rae*, based on the life of Crystal Lee Sutton, is a vivid example of the kind of bullying and intimidation women and minorities endured in the decades after World War II.

More recently, a move to flatten organizational structures emerged in the 1980s and 1990s as a result of Michael Hammer and James Champy's theories of reengineering. Organizational charts began to look like deflated triangles with a very wide base. They mostly resulted in matrix-managed organizations that still had many levels, but rather than there being one reporting structure leading up to the CEO, an employee's boss changed depending on the project to which he or she was assigned. This meant that employees often reported to several different managers. Managers in turn had a variety of teams whose members were sometimes borrowed from another line of reporting for a specific project. With workers seen as movable parts in a complex matrix, it was easy to have bullying behavior go unnoticed or be dismissed if it was reported. It was easy for a bully to hide in plain sight without drawing scrutiny.

Globalization also created enormous changes in the workplace. The speed of change in business, particularly with the constant advances in technology and the flattening of the organizational structure, resulted in a workplace that was often stressful and intense. As massive layoffs in all kinds of companies became routine, workers at all levels no longer felt secure in their jobs.

In this kind of environment, bullying can flourish. Managers and leaders may use aggressive tactics to retain control. People at every level of an organization may exhibit bullying traits as a way to undermine others while making themselves feel more secure.

And sometimes bullying behavior turns violent. According to the National Institute for Occupational Safety and Health (NIOSH), violent acts include physical assault and threats of assault. Workplace assaults range from 23,540 to 25,630 annually and are increasing.[17] And in a survey conducted in 2005 by the U.S. Department of Labor Bureau of Labor Statistics regarding workplace violence prevention, nearly 5 percent of the 7.1 million private industry business establishments questioned had an incident of workplace violence within the 12 months before the survey.

Bullying seems to occur more often in a workplace that has people in highly ranked jobs working alongside those with a lower status, according to the WBI. Healthcare, public service industries, and educational institutions seem to report more incidents of bullying. Organizations with rigid hierarchical structures, with stressful conditions, and with a bureaucratic modality, such as law enforcement, higher education, and nursing, also have seen an uptick. The more an industry feels the stress of inequity and bleak horizons for opportunities, the greater the bullying incidents.

Today workplace bullying is on the rise. A recent study conducted by the Society for Human Resource Management (SHRM) revealed that 51 percent of organizations hear about bullying incidents, citing mostly verbal abuse, malicious gossiping, and spreading lies and rumors, and 50 percent hear about bullying as the use of threats and intimidation.[18] In their book *The Cost of Bad Behavior: How Incivility Is Damaging Your Business and What to Do About It*, management professors Christine Pearson and Christine Porath provide much evidence that bullying and incivility are more manifest now because of increases in cyberbullying.[19] In the new 24/7 workplace, enabled by technology and round-the-clock communication, it is easier for bullies to survive and proliferate.

FOUR TYPES OF WORKPLACE BULLIES

As executive coaches, we listen daily to our clients' stories of bullying that they have either witnessed or suffered in the workplace—in the public sector as well as in the private sector, in the financial industry, pharmaceuticals, healthcare, technology, telecommunications, entertainment, law, government, nonprofits, and many others.

Bullies are pervasive. They demean, diminish, defame, belittle, lie, spread rumors, act selfishly, and target individuals repeatedly. Bullies have great difficulty listening, empathizing, attending, and showing respect to others in interpersonal exchanges. They usually have their own selfish agenda in mind and not the agenda of the business or company at which they work. They feel *no* remorse if their actions, such as consistently badgering subordinates, spreading false gossip, outright lying, blocking colleagues from getting credit for work, and crushing someone in a conversation, cause emotional harm.

The manifestation of bullying behavior is enhanced greatly when someone is in a position of power over others. In an October 2016 *Harvard Business Review* article titled "Managing Yourself: Don't Let Power Corrupt You," University of California, Berkeley, Professor Dacher Keltner presented a study in which he found that people in positions of power were three times more likely than those without power to yell, say insulting things, and exhibit rash, rude, and unethical actions in the office. The power differential lends itself to abuse. Drs. Ruth and Gary Namie report that 81 percent of workplace bullies are bosses or managers.[20] Without a policy of accountability for fair and respectful treatment of women and men at work, the workplace can be a potentially slippery slope where managers, plagued with insecurity and a lack of skills in civility, may fall into interpersonal bullying behavior.

We have found bullies in the workplace to fall into four common types: the Brutes, who use aggressive, antisocial, and even threatening behavior to keep others in line; the Braggarts, who are self-adoring narcissists who focus attention on themselves; the Blockers, who denigrate and always finds fault with the ideas of others; and the Beliers, who besmirch others behind their backs with false statements, rumors, deceptions, and innuendos. In developing this schema of four types of bullies, we drew on our seasoned executive coaching experience, our own research, and our knowledge of psychology.

The Belier

The Beliers slander and deceive others through lies, gossip, and rumors. Beliers misrepresent the truth behind the back of a target. They dismiss or belittle a target's contributions with false, vague, and general comments to others behind the scenes. The comments are designed to discredit the work of the target and to taint the target as incompetent and unworthy of praise. Beliers are often motivated by their own insecurity and lack of confidence, but they also can be motivated by reckless ambition, mood swings, territorialism, and resistance to change.

The Blocker

Blockers, who bully compulsively, seek to have total control over task functions at work. The Blocker creates rigid unwritten rules for others to follow, and if they don't follow them, the Blocker will discourage, dissuade, and deny others the ability to contribute their ideas. Blockers mistakenly strive for perfection by means of obsessive control over the task to the exclusion of others' impact by blocking them from participation. Their mode of operation at work is always basically the same: a serious focus on the task by placing a premium on controlling their own emotions and repelling other people's emotions. They insist that others follow a robotic method of operation in the completion of tasks without sharing how they think or feel about the work. Only the Blocker will decide what is right.

The consequence of this way of doing things is an overemphasis on details, rules, standards, and schedules. The larger goals are missed because Blockers don't see the forest for the trees. They overanalyze a task to the point of paralysis. What makes this behavior bullying is its severe exclusion of a humanistic, encouraging, and affiliative style of interpersonal relations and an overwhelming inflexibility to be open to others' points of view. This emotional deficit prevents an interpersonal relationship from developing with the Blocker.

The Braggart

A Braggart is a self-adoring and self-absorbed narcissist who seeks to inflate his own self-image. He controls others primarily through long-winded soliloquies about himself and by keeping the focus on him. We are using the male pronoun here for a reason. According to Wendy T. Behary, the founder and clinical director of the Cognitive Therapy Center of New Jersey, who maintains a private practice specializing in narcissism, and other experts in the field, more than 75 percent of narcissists are male.

One explanation is that men have a larger amygdala than women. (This is a part of the brain that triggers a competitive quest for dominance and aggression.) Although women can be narcissistic as well, they generally express it differently through an obsession with their personal appearance or the status of their children.

Braggarts have an insatiable need to be the center of attention, which, in itself, limits the capacity to be empathic or remorseful. The Braggart may not yell and scream to show his superiority but will smother others' contributions by expressing an overly inflated sense of self. He will insert, assert, intrude, decree, dictate, and declare *his* opinion or experience on a subject matter even if he knows nothing about it. A Braggart suppresses other people's creativity and prevents them from developing and maintaining a healthy sense of self and personal self-worth.

The Brute

The Beliers, Blockers, and Braggarts have a negative, toxic effect on others in the workplace. They poison morale and reduce productivity, but we believe the Brute is the most dangerous and damaging to people and to the organization. This type of bully uses antisocial, overly aggressive, and brutish behavior to dominate others with blatant disregard for their rights and sometimes safety. Brutes bully viciously and consistently to the point where their target stops performing, leaves the company, or suffers mentally and physically. Brutes create fearful, antisocial, and unproductive work environments. Their behavior can cause severe psychological and emotional distress. Brutish behaviors violate all appropriate standards of civil behavior at work.

SOCIOPATHS: INTROVERTED OR EXTROVERTED

We all have within ourselves the capacity to be overly assertive, critical, and impatient from time to time because it is in our nature. In centuries past we had to act in aggressive ways to protect or defend ourselves for survival. Bullying is different. Bullying is grounded in a need for self-gratification to shore up feelings of fear; insecurity; low self-esteem, self-worth, and self-confidence; poor interpersonal skills; and a lack of maturity and confidence.

The bullies' skewed persona has emerged from their basic temperament, their past life experiences, and the cultural influences to which they were exposed. It is also very possible that they have endured a traumatic experience in the past that has had a major influence on them.

The bullies' persona develops from the influence of the internal and biological tendencies of their temperament:

- Introverted bullies tend to be moody Beliers or controlling Blockers.

- Extroverted bullies tend to be talkative Braggarts and aggressive Brutes.

Realizing this difference is important as it determines your response. Whereas the introverted types require a patient, honest, paced, and prudent mode of communication, the extroverted types may require that the targets become more assertively extroverted themselves.

What to Expect from Introverted and Extroverted Bullies

Introverts are better at delaying gratification than extroverts. Delaying gratification is an essential life skill because it helps people better manage themselves. Introverts can have good social skills. Beliers and Blockers will be more likely to hear what it is the target needs to say as opposed to Braggarts and Brutes, who probably will respond much more quickly and parry aside or deflect the conversation.

Upon making a mistake, introverts are likely to carefully slow down to investigate how that happened, whereas extraverts speed up and don't dwell on the past. Extroverts are more interested in a fast way of problem solving or decision-making. There is a better chance of getting the necessary behavior change from the Belier and the Blocker than from the Braggart or the Brute.

Other differences include the following:

- Introverts are contained, whereas extroverts are gregariously expressive.

- Introverts are conceptual, whereas extroverts are practical.

- Introverts may accommodate information, whereas extroverts question it.

- Introverts feel and perceive, whereas extroverts think and judge.

The Blend of Brute and Braggart

The Braggart and the Brute are both extroverted and have behaviors that mesh. Many times bullies will employ both types of bullying in their behavior. The blend of Braggart and Brute consists of overtalkative, self-absorbed, and vain people who are also blunt, angry, antisocial, and emotionally impulsive. They are not aware of and do not care about their negative impact on others' sensitivities or job performance or the reputation of the company.

If the bully is a Brute 75 percent of the time and a Braggart 25 percent of the time, use tips for engaging the Brute first, but be ready to bring in your understanding of the Braggart as well. If it is 50/50, then start with the type that has caused the greater number of incidents and script out a plan for both types of engagement.

The Blend of Belier and Blocker

You may encounter the blend of the Belier and the Blocker. Both are introverted with very deep insecurities about their position in the workplace, and they have a strong need to control the work environment. There is a greater possibility of a better relationship resulting from confrontation with the Belier, Blocker, and Braggart than with the Brute. This is mostly due to the inability of the Brutes to control their anger.

CHARACTER DEFICITS OF THE FOUR TYPES OF BULLIES	
BELIER	*Does not* practice honesty, fairness, mutual respect, or sincerity with others and is not genuine in promise keeping as a result of being indifferent, ambivalent, and unremorseful about causing harm to others. **Greatest fears:** Being vulnerable and being perceived as jealous *(continued)*

BLOCKER	*Does not* practice openness, agreeableness, generosity, nondefensive listening, good interpersonal skills, humility, sound judgment, and strength of mind when dealing with the emotions of others. **Greatest fears:** Dealing with emotions and losing control of work
BRAGGART	*Does not* practice self-honesty and openness to feedback. Lacks genuine self-confidence, empathy, compassion, politeness, and team-building skills. Has no regard for the rights of others, especially if they hold different opinions or points of view. Refuses to show deference to the intrinsic and personal worth of others or refuses to listen to others. **Greatest fears:** Losing approval, prestige, or status and being rejected outright
BRUTE	*Does not* practice impulse control of emotions, delay of gratification, or patience when dealing with others. Lacks emotional strength for ego management and self-discipline. Does not monitor impact of anger on others and abuses power. **Greatest fears:** Being seen as powerless or being tricked by others

STANDING UP FOR YOURSELF

When you doubt your power,
you give power to your doubt.
—Anonymous

When you are being bullied, the workplace can feel like the loneliest place in the world. To make matters worse, you may feel powerless to do anything about it. All too often you aren't sure what to do. Standing up to a bully is a scary proposition requiring emotional fortitude. This chapter will reveal what holds targets back from standing up for themselves, how to self-assess and fortify personal confidence skills to confront a bully, how to document incidents of bullying, how to determine the type of bully you are dealing with, and what to consider when arranging the meeting to confront a bully and remedy the situation. If you are not prepared with this information, it could go terribly wrong, as it did for Greta.

Greta's Story

When Greta started her new job as the executive director of financial analysis for a midsize financial services company, she was optimistic and excited by the prospect of working for a prestigious organization where she reported directly to Burt, the CFO. He had charmed her during the interview when he described how the organization's success depended on the finance department working as a team. The other team members—two women and four men—had seemed thrilled about her coming on board during the interviews, but once she started, they seemed somewhat standoffish. She attributed this to her being the new kid on the block who hadn't yet proved herself. Greta also noticed that Burt's engagement with her had become more formal, unlike the casual communication style he had displayed during the hiring process. She worked hard to get up to speed, understand the issues, and make a contribution—even putting in extra hours on the weekend to shorten her learning curve.

Greta did much of her work independently, but the department met each week for an update and planning discussion. From the very first team meeting, Greta noticed that Burt seemed to be consistently annoyed with one or another member of the group. She observed that he became agitated about any new ideas, especially those about emerging technology. He also made sarcastic comments when he either disagreed with someone or was bored. Despite these perceptions, Greta didn't think there was a real problem, at first.

At the weekly meeting, about six weeks after Greta's arrival at the company, Burt really lit into Gordon, who was the most senior member of the team. Gordon had begun to present an idea different from the team's—that is, Burt's—current thinking. Burt became visibly angry, and he spent the rest of the meeting ridiculing and demeaning Gordon.

As Burt continued to browbeat Gordon, Greta realized that he was not only insulting Gordon but punishing everyone present with his hour-long tirade about their inability to comprehend where he was headed. As Burt continued to yell, the entire team became very quiet and passive, their eyes focused on the conference table in front of them, and no one said a word. They seemed utterly paralyzed. Their unwillingness to interrupt and defuse the situation in some way and Burt's inability to curb his own anger concerned Greta, but she did not say anything to anyone about the incident. She thought about discussing it with Lucia, whose office was next door to hers and who seemed a bit friendlier than the rest of the department, but she didn't really know what she could say. She was beginning to think that maybe there was more going on than she realized. She reminded herself that she was new and needed to keep her head down for now.

But then it happened, again—to her.

In the weekly meeting, Greta suggested another way of looking at a sensitive issue. She'd barely started her sentence, "I believe there is another way to look at this issue. In my opinion . . ." when Burt pounced on her. It became a moment frozen in time. Greta felt as though her breathing and heart rate stalled for a moment, but even more disconcerting, her thinking process became paralyzed by her embarrassment. Burt began to berate her for her failure to accomplish anything significant on the job. The words he used to attack her—"all promises, no follow-through," "empty pantsuit," "I should have known you would be a disappointment," "You are not responsive to the mission here," "How much time do you need to get it?" "You should return your sign-on bonus"— completely humiliated her. Each insult chipped away at her self-confidence. She felt drained of energy, and each time she tried to begin a defense, his voice got louder to prevent her from interrupting him. Even worse, her entire department witnessed Greta's sitting there submitting to Burt's harangue, unable to say anything.

Burt's tirade ended after 20 minutes, and the meeting adjourned without addressing all the agenda items. No one ever came to Greta's defense. The entire team flew back to their individual offices and closed their doors, Greta included. She was devastated. She couldn't think of any justification for Burt's anger. She'd been at the company for six months and by any standard was doing quite well, meeting her goals and deadlines. Later, she realized that it was just her "turn" that day. But knowing that didn't dispel the embarrassment she felt at being unfairly singled out for no valid reason or her fear of losing her new job. As time went on, things didn't get better.

In the months after that first tirade, Burt hardly talked to Greta and vice versa. They only initiated necessary conversations that were to the point and quickly dispatched so each could get away from the other. There was neither an apology from Burt nor an attempt to clear the air by Greta. She recognized that her relationship with Burt needed resetting, but she feared another blowup if she attempted to deal with the incident. Instead, it just sat there in her awareness, the elephant in the room, collecting dust, as precious time for repair ticked on. What was she supposed to do? Her boss was a bully.

Greta sensed intuitively that on some level, Burt wanted someone to be able to push back on his bullying tendencies. But she did not want to fight with him, which is the only way she could imagine engaging with his bullying behavior. Greta feared an even more volatile response if she confronted Burt, which left her with two choices: grinning and bearing it or leaving the company. She refreshed her résumé, kept her head down, suffered several more humiliations, and lasted another six months before she found another job and resigned. Burt never attempted to talk her out of leaving but used her departure as a signal to others on the team that "they could suddenly be gone too." After Greta left the company, Burt would drop her name occasionally so others would remain fearful about their own future. In team meetings if someone presented an idea that he didn't like, he would say, "That sounds like a suggestion that Greta would have made, and we all know what happened to her," as if there was more to Greta's resignation than her finding a new job.

Burt was a Brute, and he wanted a team that was fully attentive to his emotional needs. He felt threatened by anyone who brought up an idea that was different from his own; he interpreted it as a challenge to his authority. Whenever he was stressed, he vented and browbeat his department. Greta often wished she had had a face-to-face conversation with him about this behavior when she first observed it, but she felt it was too late once she became a target. After the encounter, she not only felt diminished but also couldn't help harboring a great dislike for Burt. If she had known how to deal with a bully boss, she would have taken action, but she didn't feel she had the know-how to go about confronting him without being fired. For her, leaving the job was the only way to deal with this situation.

This is a classic case of a bully's tone and behavior infecting an entire team. Burt abused his power. He didn't seem to care about his impact on others. He lacked empathy to understand where someone was coming from, listening skills to hear what the members of his team were really saying, and the ability to attend to the needs of others by encouraging the team to be thoughtful. No one in the finance department had the courage or desire to cross Burt or to try to address his behavior after one of these incidents. Likewise, his superiors avoided talking to Burt about his bullying tactics, and although human resources was aware of the problem, nothing was done.

It is easy to understand why Greta did what she did, but she might have changed the outcome of her situation—and so can you. Whether you are the victim of workplace bullying, you have a manager who is a bully on your team, or you are a leader who wants to ensure that bullying never happens in your organization, you can help stop it and prevent it from occurring in the first place. Knowing how to stand up to a bully benefits your self-confidence and self-esteem.

What could Greta have done differently to stand up for herself and deal with this Brute? A detailed account of how to deal with any Brute is in Chapter 6, but the mental preparation Greta could have considered to deal with Burt is below. These preparations would be the same no matter which of the four types of bully you were engaging.

CONSIDER WHAT'S HOLDING YOU BACK FROM STANDING UP FOR YOURSELF

According to the WBI, 56 percent of employers deny, discount, or rationalize bullying in the workplace and *only* 16 percent of employers acknowledge its existence and condemn it. This lack of general recognition and support from management could very well be the reason the target of a bully feels like the workplace is the loneliest place in the world. It could also be the reason that targets hold themselves back from taking a stand against bullies—because they know management will probably not help the situation and they, themselves, don't know how to deal with it.

Wanting to Avoid Conflict and Confrontation

Here are things to think about when you are dealing with being bullied:

- If you know that you are indeed being bullied, you must take action. If the action you choose is to do nothing and simply accommodate the conflict caused by the bullying, *and* you abandon any attempt to confront it, aside from the great resentment you will feel, this choice has a high probability to cause emotional, psychological, and physical distress.

- Do not turn your back on your values, beliefs, and personal sense of self-worth and suffer the distress and disease that come with bullying. Act responsibly for yourself. If you give up on yourself, you give away your personal power, and you will neglect your responsibility to protect yourself. If you don't stand up for yourself, don't be surprised if you are bullied at the next company. Also, acquiescing will reward the bully and will encourage him or her to bully more frequently. If you don't want to confront the bully for yourself, do it for the sake of the next target.

- Conflict is a part of the confrontation process. It may be hard to entertain the idea that the bully can change, but that is a possibility, however unlikely. Importantly, the target must exemplify and model the standard for civil interaction in dealing with and confronting the bully. Conflict can be a mere disagreement resulting from honest differences that emerge in thought and action. Learning how to get through normal conflict is part of team development. Some of the practices we discuss in this book on how to deal with bullies can be used for dealing with the normal kind of conflict. It requires patient, respectful, and honest ways of behaving with each other. Dealing with conflict might seem difficult and challenging, but if you resolve the conflict, it has a powerful effect of bringing people closer together.

- Conflict instigated by a bully is more severe; it is an expression of efforts to seize control over you as a target or the tasks for which you are responsible. The bully does so repeatedly with any combination of forceful language, impatience, coercion, and provocation. The intensity and focus one needs to deal with a bully is much more stressful than normal conflict. It requires emotional strength, tenacity, and integrity. You are vying to have your voice heard and to maintain a balance of personal and interpersonal power.

Reasons why some people tend to avoid any conflict and confrontation include the following:

- A desire to avoid exposure to the possibility of criticism and/or rejection

- A fear of social isolation or being seen as socially unappealing

- A fear of being shamed further by the bully

- An unwillingness to have the intensity of the spotlight turned on them

- An insecurity that being exposed will cause them to be seen as a fraud or in some way inadequate

- An aversion to changing anything for fear of failure, retaliation, or termination

- A lack of confidence in their interpersonal skills

- A fear of abandonment, even from the bully

- Feelings of helplessness

If you see yourself in the list above, you *must get off it now* and *get over it*. Here's how.

Assess your social capital. Develop a list of mentors, sponsors, and stakeholders who have supported you and your work at the company in the past. Ask yourself the following:

- "Have they placed or expressed value in my skills and contributions?"

- "Would they be concerned about what is happening?"

- "Can I enlist their support?"

If your research identifies some key stakeholders in the organization whose advice, counsel, and support will help you plan the appropriate next steps, set up a meeting with them. The documentation method called the Critical Incident Technique (CIT) (discussed later in this chapter) will help you prepare an objective and unemotional presentation of your situation.

Appreciate your natural interpersonal skills to defend yourself. Have you ever received feedback on your ability to get along with others? If so, what are some examples of when you have been particularly effective in dealing with difficult people? What skills were you using then that worked for you? Think about how you can apply these skills to the current situation. Remind yourself of how you have been successful in the past.

Resist getting emotional. What is the bully tapping into that is triggering your feelings of inadequacy, isolation, or despair? Appreciate that you are OK and it is the bully who has the problem. Develop positive self-talk techniques that you can employ when being bullied. For example: remind yourself that you are strong and capable and you will not let the bully define you. And walk away or excuse yourself before the bully sees you break down.

Plan confidently for the confrontation. Using the following chapters as a guideline, write out your critical incidents. Document the behaviors you want to address and script your conversation with the bully. Choose the date, time, and setting for your confrontation. You are in charge now.

Consider the alternative. Remind yourself that if you do nothing, the bully has won, and the bullying will continue. You will feel worse, your colleagues may think you are weak, and your only recourse will be to move to another job or leave the organization. If there is another valuable role for you to play elsewhere in the organization, now is the time to put that plan into action. Otherwise, gaining the strength within yourself to confront the bully is your best option.

Misunderstanding Conflict and Confrontation

Taking a stand against a bully involves confrontation. Confrontation is *not* fighting, retaliating, or expressing the aggression, anger, bigotry, unconscious bias, prejudice, immaturity, or insecurity that the bully is showing you. Confrontation is engaging the bully in a direct, specific, polite, nonthreatening, and firmly positive way. It is *not* getting even. It is resetting the relationship so that both the target and the bully can move to a place of mutual productivity at work and respectfulness in their work relationships—which will increase the amount of confidence others have to speak up and voice their ideas.

When you become an employee in a company, you do not give up your human rights. You maintain the freedom to address any behavior that is directed and destructive to you or others, for that matter. A colleague of ours says, "If you are not part of the solution, you are part of the problem." If you are being bullied and you do nothing, you must take some responsibility for allowing it to continue. The first step is to determine if the conflict is real and not just a misperception.

One way to help you determine if you are being bullied is to answer these questions:

- Is your interaction with the alleged bully intentionally negative on his part?

- Is it persistently repeated, often in front of others?

- Does it diminish your ability to work?

- Is she taking credit for your work?

- Is he discounting, demeaning, and denying your work?

- Is she using disrespectful slurs and slights, aggressive facial expressions, abusive language and extreme tones of voice (yelling, screaming, swearing, unkind name-calling, or using demeaning nicknames); pointing at you with her finger; and overall creating a hostile workplace?

- Do you feel isolated from the alleged bully and others at work?

- Does his behavior cause fear and/or loss of productivity in others at work?

- Does the alleged bullying violate principles of civility at work, such as these?

  - Lack of integrity

    - Making false, misleading, or deceptive statements

    - Acting with dishonesty, unfairness, and a lack of good faith or a failure to keep promises

- ° Lack of responsibility

  - ▸ Acting in ways that are in conflict with everyone's best interests

  - ▸ Abusing power in work relationships

  - ▸ Acting improperly and causing unethical dilemmas and mistrust

  - ▸ Acting in a way that brings harm to the person, department, division, company, and community

If you answered yes to most of the questions above, you are being bullied. If you do decide to confront him, please know that you have *the right* to do so. The bully has traveled past the boundaries of acceptable behavior. He needs to be informed of the appropriate boundaries and your expectations for civility at work.

Not Wanting to Hurt the Bully's Feelings

That's right. You don't want to hurt the feelings of the person who is bullying you. There is some logic in this. Even though you may be the target of the bully, you choose to adhere to your own principles of civility, which are based on doing no harm. The consequence of doing nothing is that you give the advantage to your bully while she is having a field day at your expense. Your virtue and, by extension, your rights are being contested, and you are not defending them. There is harm being done to you and others. You need to act on principle. Therein lies the solution. You can confront the bully, and the confrontation may adjust the playing field and possibly eliminate the nonvirtuous behavior, leading to positive productivity at work.

Hoping the Bully Will See the Error of His or Her Ways and Stop Bullying

Barbara Pachter, in her book *The Power of Positive Confrontation*, reminds us of several key points.[1] First, the target is operating on the mistaken belief that the inappropriate behavior of the bully will stop as soon as the bully understands it is inappropriate behavior. What happens, in fact, is that the inappropriate behavior escalates because it is reinforced by inattention to the behavior, and the bully sees nothing wrong with it.

This is a situation in which the bully needs to learn that his bullying is unacceptable *via feedback from the target*. The more the behavior is allowed to exist, the more likely it will continue and possibly become a part of the culture. Worse, the behavior will become a habit for the bully. The more he bullies, the more it is ingrained in his consciousness. Over time, the damage caused by the bullying will become the norm. The only way to stop that is to have coworkers begin to replace the bullying behavior with civilized behavior. The more the virtues of patience, prudence, honesty, integrity, and respectfulness in relationships replace the bullying habits of old, the greater the productivity boost at work. People will be empowered to operate from a place of confidence and strength, knowing they are acting justly for the long-term value of the company.

Fearing Being Disliked and/or Not Accepted

A desire for inclusion at work is a very real incentive that prevents people from speaking up about the bullying they witness or even when they are the target of bullying themselves. The incentive is based on the belief that if they endure the bullying without opposing it, they will become included. If they oppose it, they will be rejected by those the bully interacts with at work.

The choice to fit in has been one many of us have made at some time in our careers, most often because we needed the job to provide for our family. Not many would want to oppose bullying when there is the threat of losing their jobs. A bully can imply a threat like that, but in reality, if you are doing what you are expected to do, getting the results you were charged to get and sharing those with others, it is very difficult to get fired. It is more likely that the bullying is preventing you from performing at your best anyway, so again, *you must do something about it.*

Remember, if the bully tries to fire someone unjustly, she could very well lose her job too. The bully usually counts on the fear of job loss to get away with her immature behavior. If the targets are fearful and tolerate being bullied, the imaginary threat of the loss of the job can loom in their perception, even when that is not the reality of the situation. The targets must indicate what they are unwilling to tolerate. The bullying behavior will not change on its own if not addressed.

We suggest a direct way to stand up for yourself to any type of bully without offending or bringing retaliation upon yourself. If you tolerate the bullying, it will increase. If you push back by accusing, threatening, or judging, you can expect retaliation. But if you communicate in a calm, respectful way what your needs are to do your best work and what your boundaries are, you will build up your own self-esteem and confidence, as well as reveal to the bully the common ground upon which both of you can coexist. Of course, you can't control her reaction, but you can control yours.

Not Realizing That Employees
Are Allowed to Speak up at Work

It may seem silly to even bring up this point, but when people are hired into a multilayered business, industry, agency, or non-profit organization, they feel like they have just entered the belly of something much bigger than themselves. Many people in a large company feel the size of the structure, and they automatically go into listening, watching, and learning mode, as opposed to a more involved and energetic mode.

The choice to be in a receiving mode, as opposed to an engaging mode, is more likely to occur among the introverted population. That is why we suggest that all people learn to be an ambivert, using both their introversion and their extroversion at work. When we coach on this point, we show people who might be newly hired or newly promoted how to ease into being an ambivert. One suggestion we often use with our clients is the Three-Meeting Rule.

THE THREE-MEETING RULE

Your silence at meetings can leave a poor impression. If your name comes up in a meeting when you are not present and no one knows who you are, that too leaves a poor impression. Assumptions can be made about your silence or your lack of engagement, such as you are "out of your depth," you have "little to offer," or you are "not interested in the meeting." From your side, you are working hard to understand exactly what is going on, but others won't see that. So you must engage, and one way of doing that easily is using our Three-Meeting Rule. This is also a great way to increase your social capital and enhance your reputation and credibility.

Every meeting has three meetings within it. There is the *pre-meeting*, which is the *first meeting*, during which time some people show up earlier than just on time with the intention of engaging with the people present. This is usually about 10 to 15 minutes before the official start of the meeting. This is a time to go around the table, shake hands, introduce yourself to those you don't know or don't know well, and deepen the work relationship with others. This is often when the real agenda of the meeting is discussed and the participants get a sense of where everyone stands on the critical issues being reviewed. Never just sit down, pull out a notebook or your phone, and start working on something.

The *second meeting* is *the meeting itself,* at which you need to offer your input so that people hear your voice. This does two things: first, it shows you have a voice and are willing to use it, and second, the next time they hear your voice at a meeting, they will already be familiar with who you are. Do not wait to speak until the end of the meeting; by then it is probably too late. Participants will be anxious to finish the meeting. If you don't speak at all, others may view you as passive or having nothing substantive to add. Think in advance about what you want to say on an issue, and express your opinion or idea early in the meeting.

The *third meeting* is the *post-meeting*, after the meeting has officially ended. Some people often will stay behind to chat and debrief the meeting. It is worth it to stay for another 10 to 15 minutes, within which time real opinions about the official meeting will emerge. This is valuable information and could reveal much about the direction of the agenda points. This is when to speak up about what you learned in the official meeting and to ask questions about what you want to learn more about. You will be seen as confident and engaged, and you will be less likely to be bullied. By the way, scheduling back-to-back meetings will make using the Three-Meeting Rule difficult, so take control of your schedule too!

PREPARE FOR MEETINGS

Here are some ways to prepare for meetings through self-assessing and fortifying personal confidence skills.

Understanding Self-Other Interactions

In today's global workplace, it is becoming increasingly important to be able to understand self-other relationships at work. *Self-other relationships* simply refers to the interaction of people at work. Not so simple are the mechanics at play in those interactions. Basically, how we feel about ourselves and how we relate to others is differentiated from how others feel within themselves as well as how they relate to us. It is being aware of your own needs, wants, and insecurities as well as being aware of others' needs, wants, and insecurities. If you are able to reflect on the dynamic between these two vantage points, you will be better able to interact, negotiate, and collaborate with others. It is especially important for a person to have reflected on the power of relationships and have a mature understanding of the interaction of self and other before he or she accepts a senior position over others at work.

When bullying occurs, the bully is acting out of his own self-interest. The bully is unable and not mature enough to assess his own feelings of insecurity, much less the sensitivities of the target, and he believes his negative impact on the target is correct and justified. Moreover, he may feel that this is the best way to inspire and motivate others.

Understanding your self-concept will help you decipher the self-other relationship, which is important before you engage a bully. Your *self-concept* is a combination of how you view yourself, your feelings, and your thoughts. It is about your strengths and areas yet to be developed and a stable set of perceptions you hold important, such as what you value, like, dislike, and believe. This self-concept develops and results from feedback from others, social comparisons with others, cultural influences, and your own interpretation of the data. For our clients, we begin this self-concept exploration using an in-depth career interview.

We ask our clients to reflect on questions such as these:

- When you were young, what did you aspire to be?

- Who were your most important mentors and sponsors? What impact did they have on you?

- Describe the influence your mother and father had on you.

- Once you were an adult, how did you make your job and career choices?

- Where do you want to end up in your career?

- Describe the relationship you have with your reports, colleagues, peers, bosses, and other important stakeholders.

- When were you most satisfied with your career, and what were you doing?

- When were you least satisfied with your career? What were you doing? What did you do about it?

- When did you first move from manager to leader?

- How would you like to be described as a colleague and a leader?

- What's the one thing you won't compromise on?

These questions take us to important conversations about what is important to our client and what she most values in the workplace. We then collect 360 feedback in interviews from at least eight other colleagues to identify the gap between what the person perceives about her leadership and the collective perception of the person from others who have observed her at work. The data provides a base-rate understanding of the self, how the person typically interacts with others, what styles are working effectively, and which ones the person must change or enhance to be more successful with others. We use combinations of a number of instruments: DISC, Hogan Assessment Systems, Life Styles Inventory (LSI), and the NEO Personality Inventory (PI-R).

The DISC Style Analysis assesses behavioral intelligence at work. It is based on William M. Marston's book titled *Emotions of Normal People*.

The Hogan Assessment Systems are distributed by Hogan Assessments, Tulsa, Oklahoma. The Hogan demonstrates the link between personality and organizational effectiveness.

The LSI, a self-description of your interpersonal styles, is distributed by Human Synergistics International.

NEO PI-R, an inventory showing a five-factor model of personality, is distributed by Psychological Assessment Resources, Lutz, Florida.

These excellent assessment tools assist us in helping her understand her self-concept, what motivates her behavior, and what principles she most highly values. (Reviews of each of these instruments are detailed in the Appendix of this book.)

To further understand and appreciate a client's strengths, we conduct a skills assessment of his top accomplishments. By assessing the major skills and strengths a person uses in his top accomplishments at work, we achieve two goals: we remind the person how accomplished he really is, and we develop an excellent list of strengths that will help our client better describe and defend himself. This exercise is particularly helpful for a person who is being targeted by a bully and who may have forgotten his value proposition and self-worth. This assessment is also detailed in the Appendix. It is highly recommended for anyone who is being bullied to complete the exercise to rebuild lost self-esteem and confidence.

Confrontation is never easy, so knowing yourself and your readiness is important, as is knowing whether confrontation is safe. The following list is an adaptation from the research and writings of Christine Pearson and Christine Porath, coauthors of *The Cost of Bad Behavior*. Ask yourself these questions before you confront the bully:

- Do I feel safe talking with the bully?

- Did it seem that the bully behavior aimed at me was intentional?

- Has the bully repeated this behavior toward me more than once?[2]

If you answered yes to all three questions, you are dealing with a bully, and confrontation is possible when you are ready. If you answered no to any of these questions, it is better to wait and continue to document critical incidents, which will be discussed below. Get additional help if you feel it may not be safe to confront him, and consider having a witness present. If you are ready to engage your bully, you must prepare for the verbal exchange.

We will now focus on the emotional preparation for the meeting and the collection of critical incidents for documentation to be used when you engage the bully. Getting yourself emotionally ready with the proper mindset to stand up to your bully will require you to examine and think about your interactions. Remember, this is a self-other interaction, and it will require you to be poised, paced, polite, and patient for the interaction. Start by answering the following questions:

- Are you certain that what is happening to you is bullying?

- Have you identified what type of bully you are dealing with?

- Have you documented your experience of being bullied by using the Critical Incident Technique? To confront the bully, you will need a list of incidents to draw upon as examples and be able to talk about how the bullying made you feel.

As you examine the answers to these questions, it is important to remember that although it feels as if the bully has all the power, all too often, he is acting out of a sense of fear, low self-esteem, or lack of confidence, and he is trying to enhance his own self-concept without merit. The bully has no doubt tested your confidence and self-esteem, and you must remind yourself that your perception of his "strength" is illusory. You will need to confront your bully with courage and resilience. Focus is critical for preparation in standing up to the bully.

Clarifying Your Purpose to Confront

Be honest with yourself. Is your driving motivation to avenge yourself by retaliating against the bully? If yes, understand that works only in the movies. In real life, practical wisdom suggests you act with poise, confidence, decisiveness, and sincere purpose and not for the purpose of retaliation.

We want to eliminate bullying from the workplace altogether and create a workplace that allows for optimal productivity and true individual development. The idea that one person can bully another and get away with it is unacceptable in this day and age. The overall purpose of dealing with bullies in the workplace is to create an environment where certain positive behaviors exist and bullying behaviors don't. The individuals who stand up to the bully must also model the behaviors necessary to create a bully-proof workplace.

Here are the positive behaviors for interpersonal dialogue and meetings at work that everyone has a right to and that should be encouraged:

- Modeling behavior to set a tone of openness, respect, and integrity

- Encouraging discourse with nonjudgmental responses

- Setting a standard of fairness for expression and group discussions

- Being attentive by listening and empathizing with all points of view

- Gatekeeping contributions with a fair and patient distribution of talking time

- Addressing factors causing negative stress in interpersonal relationships

- Ensuring that all individuals are heard by monitoring the flow of communication

- Understanding that people have differences; anticipating and appreciating various reactions

- Initiating new ideas or new ways to reframe a problem to solve it

- Seeking and giving additional information and facts for clarification

- Seeking the opinions, feelings, ideas, and values of others

- Elaborating or clarifying a task with examples or analogies

- Summarizing and acknowledging everyone's ideas and suggestions

- Summarizing and acknowledging everyone's feelings and reactions

- Comparing decisions and accomplishments against group goals

- Analyzing, discerning, and determining main blocks to progress

- Taking measured steps to eliminate difficulties preventing progress

- Testing collaboration and proximity of agreement by asking for opinions

- Listing options and voting on them

- Being alert to the four types of bullies and managing their negative behaviors

- Harmonizing and conciliating differences of opinion in public

- Mediating for compromised solutions and steps going forward

- Setting procedural rules and guidelines for meetings and discussions

- Relieving tension by using humor to drain off negative feelings

- Presenting solutions in a wider context

If people in the workplace are practicing these behaviors, there really is no room for bullying. If reinforced, these positive behaviors will not only get the bully off your and others' backs but could also be a springboard for changing behavior at work. This, in turn, will have a positive effect on the culture that helps the move toward a bully-proof workplace.

MASTERING SKILLS FOR INTERPERSONAL RELATIONS, ACCOUNTABILITY, AND POWER

Standing up to your bully is a personal challenge. If it goes well, you will see the positive results right away. You will feel relief from an unjust burden and feel good about your growth as a successful businessperson.

If it doesn't go well, it may make matters worse. Therefore, preparing and evaluating the pros and cons of the confrontation are essential. First of all, you must be sure you are not operating from resentment, anger, or fear because those emotions will throw you offtrack. Once you are certain of this, consider that standing up to a bully requires very good interpersonal skills, words, and interactions that demonstrate accountability, understanding positional and personal power, and being politically savvy. Practicing these skills will enable you to show confidence during the engagement with the bully. If you are certain you can be firm, resolute, assertive, and unwilling to back down when the first provocation occurs in the discussion with the bully, it is time to act.

Some of the countercomments from the bully during the conversation will be intended to confuse, upset, or show you a lack of interest in what you have to say. Stand your ground. All bullies will try to deny what they have done, and they will be unwilling to accept responsibility. Use your critical incidents to counter any denials. They might use projection, where they blame you or others. They might use provocation to get you to overreact. If you overreact, you will lose your footing and compromise the success of your confrontation. Stand your ground in the face of these tactics. Some bullies will verbally attack you with whatever they can think of, hoping you will back down from your purpose. Use the critical incidents and follow the script you have prepared. Some will quote history in the company as a way of showing their knowledge and diminishing the incidents of bullying as of no consequence. But it is of great significance to you, so stand firm. Others may feign innocence and play ignorant. Some may threaten you with the loss of a job just to see how serious you are. Again, stay focused. If the bullying behavior becomes threatening or violent, leave the office and go directly to security to file a report, which becomes another critical incident.

In all these situations you must remain poised and not get provoked into aggression or any kind of sarcasm. Sarcasm is very hurtful, and it will signal to the bully that you want a fight, not a resolution. The tone of your voice is a sign of your emotional state of mind. The conversation should be geared to maintaining the personal self-worth of both you and the bully. It is taking the high road. Never attack the bully's personhood, character, personality, or judgment. Never put her down. We recommend that you be nonpunishing in every way, using gravitas and the essential interpersonal skills listed below.

Listening: Confronting Your Bully Requires Listening First

Nondefensive listening helps you to take in information while searching for the real purpose of the communication, having an open mind about what is being said, hearing how it is being said, and avoiding distractions. It requires restraint, courage, and a willingness to hear the truth about the content of communication. Psychologist Dr. Karl Menninger has suggested that people magnetically gravitate toward the person who is listening to them speak.[3] Some tips for nondefensive listening are these: maintain frequent eye contact, avoid distractions, do not interrupt unless to paraphrase or ask for clarification, suspend judgment by looking for the worth of the content, be patient, and summarize the message gleaned from the speaker.

Empathizing: Be Attuned to the Inner World of the Other Person

Understanding the emotional base from which a person is speaking helps the target take a stand against the bully. *Empathy* is being attuned to the inner world of the bully but not feeling sorry for him. Sympathy is different from empathy. *Sympathy* is feeling sorry for the other person, and it may make it harder to have a genuine and objective conversation with the bully. Empathy is a powerful force in communication. Empathy allows us to hear more clearly what is really going on inside the bully. It helps us be emotionally strong and keep the needs of our ego at bay so we won't be provoked by the bully. By combining nondefensive listening and empathy, we are able to attend fully to the conversation with the bully. This will keep us on track without our own biases and preconceived ideas about the bully influencing the conversation.

Authenticating: Reclaim Your Natural Tendency to Grow

What does *authenticating* mean? It means standing up for your right to grow, develop, and progress. It is what an oppressive bully is preventing you from doing in your work. Obviously, for the bully, this natural tendency has gone awry, causing a decay of civil standards for her interactions with others. Her approach is oppressive and tends to stall the personal growth in others as well as in herself. But even as we stand up to the bully, we want to be sure we are not doing it in a way where we are blind to her essential needs. If we employ the same behaviors the bully uses in our confrontation, we bring ourselves down to her level. As we fully attend to the bully during the conversation, we want to recognize that the bully is worthy of her own personal or professional aspirations. Our complaint is the *way* the bully is behaving. We are not challenging her right to grow and aspire, however skewed her methods might be.

In attending to the bully, consider the following questions: What level of ability does the bully display? What educational and experiential background does the bully possess? What are the bully's interests, goals, values, and beliefs? What is the bully's level of need to belong to the company and to have prestige within the company? Our effort to stand up to our bully represents the fact that we are feeling thwarted in our growth and aspirations, which is affecting our productivity at work. By confronting the bully, you are simply reclaiming your right to grow authentically and develop on the job by removing the behaviors you find oppressive.

Dialoguing: Ensure Your Impact When Engaging the Bully

Usually, the practice of dialogue in communication is confused with debate, discussion, or rebuttal. Only when a problem is framed from different points of view can a true dialogue begin, with the aim of a meaningful exchange that will move the thinking beyond the understanding of any one person. In dealing with a bully, dialoguing is practiced by suspending judgment, monitoring and managing your ego to keep it in bounds, presenting the problem in a direct, specific, and nonpunishing way, and, finally, engaging for the purpose of gaining shared meaning of the solution to the problem. In the case of bullying, the change in behavior is the solution. To dialogue:

- Model give-and-take during the conversation. It is a two-way conversation in which one person speaks and the other one listens, and then the listener speaks in return, and so on.

- Stay on message until you see it acknowledged, and then strive for a new way of working together.

- Maintain an even vocal tone at a normal rate, neither too soft nor too loud.

- Maintain gesturing to a moderate level—no pointing.

- Prevent your message from being misinterpreted or interrupted.

- Present the image of a person who is not asking permission.

- Maintain a calm exterior during the confrontation.

- Be firm with facts and circumstances.

Successful dialoguing has to do with clarifying misperceptions and incongruities in communication, as well as stopping the bullying. Dialoguing can help sort all of that out. As Mary Parker Follett, considered by some to be the mother of modern management, has said, "Unity, not uniformity, must be our aim. We attain unity only through variety. Differences must be integrated, not annihilated, not absorbed." For both the bully and the target, this is true. It becomes imperative to clarify the two different perceptions.

Aligning the Verbal, Vocal, and Visual Parts of the Conversation in Your Dialogue

What will make your dialogue more dynamic is practicing the alignment of the verbal, vocal, and visual aspects of conversation. If confluent, the three parts become seamless and mutually supportive of your overall message to the bully. For the *verbal part*, the choice, sequencing, clarity, and delivery of your words in concise, short sentences are critical—but the verbal part represents only about 15 percent of the impact of your message. The *vocal part* (35 percent) refers to the vocal variety of the sound of the words we use—that is, the tone, the volume, and so on. The *visual part* (55 percent) refers to our facial expressions, eye contact, gestures, posture, movement, personal-space practices, dress, grooming, and appearance.

When all three parts are aligned and working together, the message has a higher chance of being understood. The overall projection is one of calm, conviction, confidence, and credibility. We have talked about the words, but the tone of voice is also critical. If it is too aggressive, you will create more tension. If it is too soft, passive, or whiny, you will increase your chance of being further bullied. Likewise, you have to practice your visuals. Appearing too angry, upset, or emotional can also defeat the goal of the meeting.

THE START OF THE CONVERSATION WITH THE BULLY: EXPECTED VERSUS OBSERVED

No matter which type of bully you are dealing with, the start of the confronting conversation will be the same. Explain in as few words as possible, being very specific and nonthreatening, what you expect in interpersonal behavior between members at work and what you have observed. Stating what is expected *and* what is observed quickly focuses the attention on the problem. It is the gap between what is expected and observed that reveals differences. It brings up the problem without judgment or blame and without saying, "I have a problem to talk to you about." Also it gives you confidence that you are in control of the conversation, and as long as you stay resolute to the plan of the confrontation, you will control the conversation, show your emotional strength, establish boundaries for how you want to be treated, and show you are operating from your personal power.

An Example: Stating What Is Expected and What Is Observed

You: "Mark, I expected budget support from you for the Madison project so I would be able to complete the project under budget and on time. I observed that the funds you initially identified for the Madison project were redirected to the marketing department. What happened?" (You already know that Rob, who runs the marketing department, is a long time friend of Mark. Often, Mark changes funding allocations to his favorites on the team, which is primarily made up of men. However, you don't say that.)

When Mark responds, look for an openness or a lack of it in the conversation. Is he willing to talk about it? Is he showing anger and retaliation? Is he trying to turn the topic back on you? Whatever he shows, unless it is volatile behavior, stay resolute to explain your concerns.

If he has an emotional response of frustration, reflect back the emotion, saying, "You seem frustrated! Please help me understand why." The goal here is to establish the fact that you were affected by such an important change in funding and that he cut into your area of decision-making and effectiveness. You want to show your emotional strength and then redirect the conversation by discussing a successful change that everyone can live with for the good of the business.

Remember, you have other critical incidents collected that you can use, if necessary, in this conversation. Also, remember that the bully will try to gain the upper hand by bullying even more in the conversation. Your response is to stand resolute, remain confident with emotional composure, be logical, and exhibit calm, nonthreatening behavior and much better interpersonal skills than the bully.

Documentation Method: Critical Incident Technique

It is important to document the critical incidents of the bullying behavior. The critical incidents are made up of the information that answers the questions as to what is expected and what is observed. Critical incidents are supporting proof of the problem you are articulating.

The Critical Incident Technique (CIT), originally developed by J. C. Flanagan, is a procedure for collecting, analyzing, and describing direct observations of human behavior to facilitate their usefulness in solving practical problems—which in this case are the behaviors of the bully.[4] The CIT provides derived classifications of bullying behavior from real-world examples in the workplace. We recommend the CIT for sorting out the difference between unacceptable bullying behaviors and acceptable nonbullying behaviors by using our characteristic classifications of the four types of bullies. Sometimes it is discerned that an initially observed behavior thought to be bullying turns out to be nonpunishing and nonbullying and is simply a stylistic difference in someone's behavior.

Each incident recorded must be a description of a bully's behavior. It must be sufficient to clearly define the intent of the person performing the behavior as a bully. The behavior must be from firsthand observations of a situation in which the purpose or intent seems fairly clear to the observer and the consequences are sufficiently obvious to leave little doubt concerning its effects. The three parts of each incident include a description of the situation, the behavior, and the consequence.

The purpose of the CIT is to formulate, from the many critical incidents, a comprehensive list of bullying behaviors to show repeated assaults on the target. We encourage you to record only the behavior and its effect on you, not your judgment or evaluation of the behavior. The CIT will help you recognize the type of bully with whom you must engage and confront by using our list of characteristics. Try to place specific behaviors, such as rumor mongering, lying, blocking input, slights, slurs, verbal abuse, yelling and screaming, angry and hostile facial expressions, pointing a finger, tightening a fist, and using threatening words, voice, or visual expressions, into one of the four types of bullying.

Present the difference between what is expected and what is observed:

- For example, "I love my job and this company. I work hard and am very knowledgeable in my field. I expect to have my opinions considered and treated with respect. This is the same respect I have for my colleagues. I have observed that you appear to be frustrated by my work style, disappointed by my work productivity, and angry at me when I share an opinion."

- Support your statements with the CITs so the problem is made clear. Say more about the differences. Keep the conversation going, using your emotional strength, but not by being emotional, until you are able to discern the bully's reaction, whether there is an unwillingness to have a constructive conversation or if he is not emotionally able to have one. If you show hesitation, the bully will use that to take control of the conversation, so stay resolute.

- Chances are the bully will be unwilling to engage constructively and will send signals of retaliation. At this point, list the negative consequences his behavior is having on you in the job and how others are affected by it. If you are still meeting with resistance and/or the bully is getting emotionally upset, you may want to stop the conversation and pick it up later. Otherwise, you can deal with the emotion by using this phrase, "You seem upset. Can you tell me why?"

- Remember, you have a plan, so you can anticipate his reactions with actual lines of dialogue you have scripted ahead of time. You know the bully best, so customize your plan to the bully. As you prepare the script, make sure you memorize the start (what is expected and what is observed) so it comes off as very professional.

The residual message is about the behavior that you want the bully to change. Repeat this several times to keep the focus on it. You state it when you say what is expected and what is observed. You may refer back to it at any time during the conversation, and be sure to end with it. If at all possible, try to make sure the bully understands your intention is to change the behavior you are speaking about. Intentionality, as represented in the residual message, will help you be successful in the confrontation. Don't let the bully sidetrack you.

Probe for better understanding. If you want or need more information from the bully, questions you could ask include these: "Help me gain more insight into this" and "Is there anything else I need to understand about this?" If there is a sudden increase in emotion, use this: "Help me understand why you are so concerned about this" or "You seem very concerned about this. Why?"

Paraphrasing is another interpersonal skill that keeps the conversation going so that both the target and the bully may reach common ground. Simply state what you do understand and ask for more information about what you do not understand. Paraphrasing is one way to reduce the complexity of the conversation. For example, "I understand your desire to make quick decisions and meet deadlines. I don't understand why you get angry when my research has uncovered a potentially serious issue that needs to be taken into consideration."

Write out what you believe will be the sequence of the conversation and plan where you might use the skills we have discussed. Another skill to use is to be respectfully polite by maintaining the personal worth of the bully and to stand up for yourself if she gets disrespectful. If the bully starts yelling, stand up if you are sitting, look her in the eye, use her name, and ask her to please stop yelling. Sometimes you have to show it by putting up your hand as a gesture to stop. Explain that you have common goals for the company and whereas you may have differences, you want to be able to work through those differences together for the benefit of the company. If she can't stop yelling, excuse yourself.

Even though the conversation did not turn out the way you would like, you have been successful in establishing your boundaries, standing up for yourself with resolve, maintaining your emotional composure, showing stamina, and focusing on the facts and what is best for the company. If there is a company policy against bullying, you have an official document supporting your individual attempts to stop bullying on the job. Bullies destroy fair play as they deny a company the benefit of productivity and deny the person the right to grow and develop.

KNOWING THE DIFFERENCES BETWEEN POSITION, POLITICAL, AND INTERPERSONAL POWER

There are different types of power, and it's important to understand how people use them.

Position Power

Position power is usually associated with a person's rank, named position, tenure, seniority, or connections with others who have high-level leadership roles in the company. Position power grants the holder certain responsibilities, such as hiring, placement, firing, and revamping structure. A bully can use position power by holding sanctions (hiring, placing, moving, assigning projects, disciplining, and terminating) over the heads of employees to remind them often that he has power over them, especially to end their employment.

As we have learned, 81 percent of workplace bullies are bosses who have position power over others. Bullies with position power rely on it regularly as a form of coercion. They want people to do it their way, or else. Often the person who offers other ways of doing things becomes a target. The bully may use a tone in conversation with subtle or overt threats of dismissal, create a climate of menacing fear to get things done, and degrade interpersonal skills.

Political Power and Influence

Bully bosses can be deceitful office politicians if not political animals. They are often overly political, and their behaviors poison projects and programs that do not benefit them in some way. They will take credit for everything done by others, especially to anyone in higher positions. They never credit the people who do the real thinking and work, much less praise or positively reinforce the behaviors of these workers. They care little for rules unless those rules support their selfish ends. Political power and influence are misused by these bullies. It is evident in the signs below:

- Lack of sensitivity to how work gets done

- Lack of thoughtfulness in the process of getting work done

- Continuous reneging on promises

- Taking credit for the accomplishments of others

- Failure to promote others for their value at work

- Failure to build positive internal and external networks

- Failure to bring up for open dialogue work issues

- Failure to correct issues of integrity

In comparison, appropriate political practices that use interpersonal power well are these:

- Building and maintaining key business relationships

- Giving credit to those who do the work

- Knowing and respecting the organization's cultural norms and core values

- Knowing how to get buy-in to implement positive ideas

- Being willing to challenge ideas and raise difficult issues

- Acting with integrity for the self and the organization

- Seeking feedback from others while building alliances

Interpersonal Power

When a target is standing up for herself, it is good to know the kinds of power she is dealing with and the interpersonal power she has available to use for her engagement with the bully. *Interpersonal power* is the personal power that is shown by the character and emotional strength a person brings to work and her capacity in sociability, social sensitivity, mutual respect, listening, and empathy. These skills allow the following:

- Recognition of the positive flow of productivity at work

- Treatment of all work colleagues with consideration

- Rejection of psychological, physical, and emotional abuse

- Engagement with others in a way that uplifts, inspires, and supports

- Communication with others that is inclusive of differences

A bully will try to corrupt these positive aspects of interpersonal power in you. Sometimes the bullies have poor character and interpersonal skills to begin with. They are threatened by those who have good character and interpersonal skills because these are the people who can rebuke corrupt political and position power practices. Power is not in itself corrupt.

To paraphrase playwright and economist George Bernard Shaw, it is those who do not understand how to use power well and for a positive purpose who corrupt and distort it. Bullies don't understand it or refuse to see the value of its positive use. When we take a stand against a bully, we must feel confident of our good interpersonal power skills. Balancing power with the bully is what the confrontation is all about. It is correcting his coercive and corrupt power over you. Your goal is to take your personal power back, not take his power away. It is to bring balance to the relationship.

SUGGESTIONS FOR THE MEETING WITH THE BULLY

Here are some important logistical issues you need to attend to in order to have a successful confrontation.

Where and When Will You Meet with Your Bully?

Set up a private meeting in a neutral place where you will not be interrupted. If the incident happens in a meeting or group setting, take the bully aside immediately afterward if you can and ask, "Can I see you for a minute?" Find a private space to discuss what happened. If you are brushed off, set up a time to meet as soon as possible.

Preparing a Script

Prepare a script for the conversation so that you are ready to assert your perception of the bully's behavior as recorded in your documentation of critical incidents. The script will allow you to navigate the conversation and deal with the bully's reactions. You may encounter emotional responses such as anger, sarcasm, frustration, or skepticism, and you must be ready to withstand them to achieve your goal of changing the bully's behavior toward you.

In the chapters that follow, we provide scripts that are tailored to the different types of bullying personalities and situations. In general, you should accomplish the following in preparing your script:

- Begin with your expectations about how colleagues treat one another at work.

- State what you have observed (or experienced) and the problem that you are having with the bully in a specific, nonthreatening manner.

- Include questions and statements that will allow you to address and affirm the bully's emotion.

- Suggest specific strategies for the type of bully with whom you are dealing.

- Include specific remedies that you can use to exit the conversation quickly should the bully become overly emotional or hostile.

It is always best to write down how you would ideally like to deliver the message and to include responses that you might receive. Then rehearse the conversation out loud in front of a trusted friend or colleague so that you can be more at ease. Rehearsing is important and will lead to a more confident discussion.

Your success in the prearranged, one-on-one meeting also depends on your being able to remain in control of your emotions and focused on outcomes. The final steps of your planning include being able to answer these questions:

- Do you know how you will maintain your composure during the meeting?

- When confronted, most bullies back down, but it is possible that she will deliver a few choice comments during the conversation. Remember, this is not personal, and the bully is the one with the problem, not you! Deflect the comments and bring the discussion back to the points you wish to make. Use positive self-talk to deflect the bully's harsh words. Keep yourself centered by taking slow deep breaths.

- Do you know what you want to walk away with from the meeting?

- Be reasonable with your expectations. These situations do not change overnight. You could agree that you will give the bully a silent sign when you feel victimized again so as to stop her in the moment. You could agree to meet in a week to discuss any new incidents if they occur and check on progress. If there is a true disagreement about what has happened in the past, you could agree to bring the issue to a third party, such as human resources, to discuss and agree on some preventive strategies. You might discover that you have played a role in the bullying and really need to listen to the feedback and become more aware yourself.

CATEGORIZING THE BULLY

Typically, a target should record approximately 5 to 10 critical incidents to do an analysis of the documentation. When you categorize the behaviors that occurred in each critical incident, patterns will begin to emerge that can help the target determine if the bully is a Belier, Blocker, Braggart, or Brute. Checklists for each of the four types of bullies are located at the end of each of the next four chapters. Each checklist allows you to assess what kind of bully you are dealing with.

REMINDERS

- When you stand up to the bully, be resolute.

- You do not give up your rights when you become employed. An important code of behavior in society is to be civil with each other.

- Challenging a bully requires interpersonal skill, behavioral maturity, confidence, and assertiveness, not aggression.

- Your voice is a sign of your emotional state of mind, so do not confront at a time when you are not yet in control of your emotions. You must be firm, resolute, assertive, factual, and diplomatic. Stay committed, and do not get provoked by the bully. Don't scowl or use harsh tones or angry facial expressions.

- When you are confronting the bully with your expectations and your observations, he may react emotionally. You must deal with the emotion first, before you continue your script. Engage the emotion by saying something like, "You seem perturbed. Help me understand why." Once the emotion is reduced, then you may proceed with your script and critical incidents.

- If and when you have reached a satisfactory resolution to eliminate the bullying behavior, you must assure yourself that you have compliance by asking, "So this means that I can count on a change in our interactions?" If you suspect any lack of closure, ask, "It sounds like you're really not ready to make the change. What more can we discuss to solve this difference? After all, we are on the same team."

If they have more to discuss, do it there and then. Get compliance before the meeting ends by being humble and respectful yet resolute. Listen for a truth you can both agree upon. After the heat of an exchange, try to find something genuinely positive to say to the other person. This will convey an attitude of respect. You expect respect, but you may have to model it first.

- Remember that standing up for yourself builds self-esteem and confidence and you are *the only one* who can stand up for yourself. Both your self-concept (how you see yourself) and your self-esteem (how you value yourself) will increase with every successful confrontation. Also, as you continue to do so, you will become more resilient and more able to face conflict whenever it emerges.

- If you do meet with retaliation from the bully, remain poised and polite.

- If you are brushed off, just say, "It is unfortunate you choose to think like that" or "I understand your choice to think and behave in that manner, but it is unfortunate you choose to do so."

- Never be sarcastic, as it is the most hurtful form of criticism and reveals your own inability to communicate effectively.

- Conflict is inevitable, but it doesn't have to be destructive. Confronting conflict requires a patient, respectful, and honest way of interacting with each other. At first, it always feels insurmountable, but if you persevere and resolve the conflict, it has the effect of bringing people closer together than ever.

- Do not stay silent if you experience bullying or witness it. Remember, when someone bullies and gets away with it, it only reinforces the behavior and allows it to happen again.

- Openly discuss bullying behavior and its consequences with your colleagues and team members. Review the most appropriate ways of addressing it and eradicating it. No one is born with the skills necessary to confront a conflict with a bully. It must be learned.

- Never put someone down in front of others or behind his back. Do unto others as you would have them do unto you. Confronting the bully does not mean turning into one.

- Beliers and Blockers are more introverted, and Braggarts and Brutes are more extroverted. If you are the opposite of the bully, you may have to adjust accordingly as you learn to be an ambivert.

- Cynicism, skepticism, indifference, selfishness, and self-indulgence are all rooted in immaturity and undermine positive productivity.

- Never use one of the four types of bullies as a label or an epithet for another person. Only use the categories to help you identify the type of bully with whom you are dealing.

- Set boundaries. Remember, we teach others how to treat us by what we permit and tolerate.

- Empathy is not feeling sorry for someone. It is seeing her inner world and how it influences her behavior.

- Confrontation is not retaliation. It is hard work, but it can yield a change in behavior that brings with it a great feeling of accomplishment.

- If you are a leader in your organization—whether you run a team, a department, a division, or the entire company—you are a role model, and you are being watched by and influencing others. Examine your own behavior to ensure that you do not have any tendencies toward the four types of bullies. Actively present the kind of communication and interpersonal interactions that foster cooperation and civility.

HOW TO ENGAGE THE BELIER

He who permits himself to tell a lie once,
finds it much easier to do it a second time.
—Thomas Jefferson

A Belier's intentions and actions are not always easy to detect. A Belier bullies indirectly by telling lies behind the scenes about the target. Pretty soon others get caught up in repeating the lies, which creates an insidious rumor mill within the team or organization. The Belier does more than just violate the standards of civility with regard to people at work. She creates an alternative and false perception of others.

Beliers have a twisted view and interpretation of others' actions in the workplace, which is probably a projection of their own inadequacies. Any behavior, such as a colleague's visiting his sick mother, becomes a distorted story, such as overdependence on his parents. However innocent the behavior, it will get spun into something nefarious. Respect is compromised with innuendo and slurs. The result is that the Belier's impact multiplies like viruses—and can be extremely difficult to stop. Mark Twain once remarked, "A lie can travel halfway around the world while the truth is putting on its shoes."

Beliers go through interpersonal relationships quickly because of their predilection to become suspicious of another's success. They may approach a new interpersonal relationship at work positively until person A, who at first was not seen as threatening, later poses a threat because of her competence. The threat is that person A may inadvertently expose a Belier's insecurity and incompetence. The Belier will then turn to person B to sabotage person A with gossip and rumor. This tendency to set someone up for failure behind the scenes just because the target seems to be more attractive or smarter is insidious in nature, and it can fester and spread in a work environment. Unfortunately, if the Belier's campaign is not stopped at the outset, it may escalate into the open.

Because of the Belier's mood swings, it is important to realize that there is no middle ground. A relationship with a Belier starts with observable behavior that on the surface seems supportive. The behavior then swings from falsely supportive to covertly negative behavior, so there is no room for the development of a true work relationship. The swings can be extreme and irrational. Eventually, the clandestine campaign emerges for all to see.

If a target objects to the false claims of a Belier, the Belier will besmirch the reputation of the target by defaming, disparaging, discrediting, spinning half-truths, and manipulating private information. With position power or long tenure in a company, Beliers can cause a great deal of damage to the target's career and greatly reduce productivity at work. Beliers destroy careers without feeling remorse. If your boss is a Belier, you have to be patient and resilient while collecting as many critical incidents of the bullying as possible to protect yourself. One option, of course, is moving on to another boss or job. A second option is to confront the Belier, and the third is to build support elsewhere in the company to refute the rumors. Coaching and counseling may help as well.

If you are managing and coaching Beliers, patience and documentation work in an effort to make them better-functioning team players. The reality is that they may never lose the trappings of Belier behavior; they may just do less of it if they know they are being monitored. It is better not to hire them in the first place because it is difficult to fire them; they would see a lawsuit as another opportunity to lie and to practice their type of bullying.

One Fortune 50 firm we know hired a Belier as the head of human resources. Think of that for a minute! Where else could Beliers better hide and practice their craft of passive-aggressive mischief? What amazed us was that 20 years later the person was still in the same role, having targeted numerous workers who left or were fired according to how well they dealt with the Belier. When he passed away, everyone saw an immediate change in the culture.

Another case showed how one senior person insisted that a junior person list the senior person's name on his résumé as a reference. The senior person promised to provide positive comments as the junior executive moved to another job in a larger city. The junior executive was thankful for the reference, and he did not realize for years that the senior executive was indirectly casting aspersions about the junior executive's competence whenever he was called for a reference. He would use silence in response to the question, "Would you hire him again?" which was often interpreted as a negative. How much damage was done to the younger executive will never be known.

Beliers often have these characteristics:

- A desire to harm the target without drawing attention to themselves or their own shortcomings and incompetence.

- A trigger to action from their own past feelings of incompetence, betrayal, or abandonment; difficulty controlling anger; poor self-image; mood swings; impulsivity, or emotional emptiness.

- A preference for lies, gossip, half-truths, and rumor mongering that undermine and socially isolate their target. Beliers can be selfish and petty, and they will purposely foment conflict when there is evidence that an enhanced relationship or collaboration is a desired state between a target and a coworker.

- A Belier's actions are covert and often difficult to trace back to the original source. The harm can be caused by casual comments, skeptical questions, and raised eyebrows when a target is being discussed or praised.

- Beliers enjoy spreading gossip. They will shrewdly pick up on a bit of truth and exaggerate it into a full-blown untrue story. Although initially started by them, the story is spread throughout a company by others, making it hard to trace it back to the original source. Rumors spread swiftly and leave havoc in their wake.

- Beliers rarely feel guilty about the damage they have caused to someone's reputation. Their view of the world is very self-serving. They may feel that they have brought about justice when the target is forced to leave or resign because his reputation has been damaged beyond repair.

- Beliers can appear interested in their target. They are often the first to welcome a new employee to the company or a member to the team. They will gain information from the newbie that might be useful down the road to discredit her, and they will give information on others that may not be accurate.

- Beliers have no true sense of justice or fairness; when they undermine someone's career, they don't see it as selfish or immature. They are cynical about others, causing Beliers to be indifferent. Giving a Belier a position as manager can be deadly; he is capable of causing psychological terror in a target who is a subordinate. It becomes difficult for the target to defend himself against the Belier, and this can lead to a sense of helplessness. Even more calamity can be caused by a Belier in a position of higher power, who can grievously compromise the mission of the company through lies, gossip, and rumor.

Joan's Story

Joan had been working in marketing and public relations for 10 years when a major bank called and asked her to join the marketing department. It was a dream job: her salary almost doubled. She was excited about learning from the pros at the bank, especially her new boss, Nicole, who had 25 years of experience. Joan came to work eager and willing to learn. What she didn't know was that one of her peers, Vanessa, felt very threatened by her.

Although Vanessa was friendly at first, Joan realized almost immediately that Vanessa was gossiping about Joan's past employment and spreading a tall tale about her stopping at a liquor store every day on the way home from work.

Joan ignored it and thought her work would speak for itself. Unfortunately, though, Vanessa repeated the story offhandedly in the kitchenette, ladies' room, hallways, and parking lot to anyone who would listen. Joan did not always know about it or the extent of Vanessa's stories.

Once the gossip took effect, more indirect bullying began to occur. People began avoiding Joan. Any conversation with Joan, even a casual one, was short—as if no one really wanted to invest in her as a colleague. Her boss, Nicole, started hearing the stories, but instead of investigating, she isolated Joan from any real work at the company just in case the rumors were true. Once Joan was referred to as a "drunk," that was it. Joan's reputation was severely damaged. Joan realized she was being isolated, and she knew that Vanessa was behind it. Something was very wrong, but Joan did not know what to do. Eventually, Joan was given a pink slip for low productivity, and she was left stymied and deeply hurt by the entire experience, which made no sense to her.

In dealing with a Belier, the target's goal is to discuss the problem calmly and courageously, relieve the tension, and create space for a solid working relationship. Because Beliers often bully when their target is not present, using innuendo, it is especially important to have clear evidence of their behavior. We recommend that you document critical incidents so that the bully will not be able to dismiss her sometimes subtle behavior as unintentional. Address the Belier in a nonpunishing way using the facts you have accumulated objectively and calmly.

Remember, the Belier is probably an introvert, so easygoing communication will work best. There is usually a gap between your expectations of how you should be treated and your observations of the Belier's actual conduct, which will determine the structure of the conversation. It is important to state specifically what you expect from coworkers and what they can expect from you. After you have clearly established those expectations, discuss the facts that you have collected using the Critical Incident Technique (CIT).[1] Then make sure to finish the conversation by developing a plan to address the issues you've raised.

Let's use Joan's story for documenting a critical incident and then script out how to engage the Belier.

CRITICAL INCIDENT REPORT
FOR JOAN'S STORY

Situation 1: I was eager and had high expectations and a devoted willingness to learn when hired. Within weeks of my arrival on the job, I started to feel isolated from you and other people around me. People would stop talking when I entered the break room to get some coffee.

Behavior 1: I asked one person to confide in me about the distancing I felt from others. This person shared with me the rumors about my drinking problem and how an increasing number of people were talking about it.

Consequence 1: This was a shock to me because I don't drink any alcohol at all, to which my husband can attest. But I do remember once seeing you in the distance after I entered a liquor store to buy wine for my dinner guests. I see no other connection with the false stories. As these rumors have spread, I have noticed my isolation from members of my team, you, and my boss, Nicole. People talk to me only when absolutely necessary.

JOAN'S SCRIPT

Writing a script for what you would like to say to your bully is a good way to prepare and practice. The script for the meeting should begin with what you expected and what you observed. Then you should write out how you think the bully will respond.

Joan should arrange a meeting with Vanessa in a private room or office. If the conversation with Vanessa doesn't help the situation, she can modify the script for a conversation with her boss, Nicole. For example:

> *Joan:* I really like my job and the company, and I expect to work in a culture of mutual respect and tolerance.
>
> *Vanessa:* Don't we all? So what's on your mind?
>
> *Joan:* Well, I have been informed by another person, who will not be named, that there are rumors that I have a drinking problem. [Joan should pause and wait for some kind of response before asking her directly.] Have you heard such false rumors?
>
> *Vanessa:* [Silence.]
>
> *Joan:* Is it true that there are false rumors?
>
> *Vanessa:* I really wouldn't know.
>
> *Joan:* Let me give you an example of what I am talking about. [Joan should read the documented critical incident

report. She should start by sharing Situation 1, Behavior 1, and Consequence 1 as she's written them. There should be a verbal response at this time to which she will have to remain poised and in control because the response from the Belier can be explosive. This exchange can become the second critical incident to record.]

Joan: Vanessa, I would hope that you will bring any false rumors to my attention as a heads-up, especially now that you know I do not drink alcohol. Would you agree to that, please? And will you help me defeat these rumors with the truth?

Vanessa: [We hope she agrees and does her part to stop the rumors. One thing is for sure: Joan should feel good that she has confronted her bully. The Belier has been put on notice and may not bully her again. If the Belier does agree to stop spreading the lies about her and help restore her reputation, then she can add the following sentences.]

Joan: Thank you for agreeing to help. I'd like us to work successfully together. I believe I can learn a lot from you. If we agree to listen to each other and to be honest and open with our ideas and disagreements, then I can see us meeting on a regular basis. Are you OK with meeting more often?

Vanessa: Sure. [Joan must get agreement from Vanessa. However, Beliers might agree, but they often lie. So even if the Belier says yes, you need to hold her to it so she realizes that it is an actual agreement between the two of you. For insurance, always document. Documentation is important because you can use it later to show the Belier the real words used in your critical incidents with her. Record this exchange as a second critical incident report. If Vanessa does not agree, which is unlikely because Beliers don't like to be exposed, Joan should simply say, "Help me understand why you will not agree to an arrangement that will make us both more productive at work." Joan should wait for the response and probe deeper if no reasons to agree are revealed.]

Joan: I am happy you have agreed. I look forward to our meetings and perhaps coming up with ideas for collaboration and cooperation for both of our success at the job. How about every Tuesday at 8:30 a.m. before our staff meeting?

Vanessa: All right.

Joan: I'll send a calendar invite so it's on both of our schedules.

Richard's Story

Richard was a director of human resources at a Fortune 100 manufacturing firm. He liked his sphere of influence in HR, but he wanted to expand his understanding of the company. He thought that networking in other parts of the company would increase his visibility and credibility with the leaders of the organization. He elected to network first with Darla, the vice president of marketing and communications for the firm. When Richard told Darla that he was interested in knowing more about the company, she perceived it as his impertinence and impatience to move up in the company. Darla became alarmed and insecure, which emanated from self-doubt about her competence. In addition to Richard's popularity at his level, of which Darla was envious, she was jealous that she did not think to network strategically herself. It just never occurred to her.

Out of this frustration with herself, an idea arose. Although Richard's interest in outreach was to build a wider bandwidth of understanding about the company's vision and mission, Darla's insecurity got the best of her, and she perceived that Richard was a threat. In this perfect storm of fear and jealously, Darla began a devious counterattack. She did not want anyone to know how she felt, so her silent campaign was to create doubt about Richard's motivations. She began with innuendos to others—"He only wants to move up fast"—sowing uncertainty about Richard's intentions and competence. Over the next few months, as Richard navigated the organization, meeting with key decision-makers, Darla's fear crystalized into anger, and she became more passive-aggressive. Richard asked her for an introductory meeting with Harold, the executive vice president of sales. Darla agreed.

Richard trusted Darla to present him in a positive light. Darla knew that was Richard's expectation. She had worked with Harold on many projects, and she knew what pushed his buttons. Harold disliked anyone who was not cogent and concise in conversation. Richard was laid-back, easygoing, a bit vague in conversation, and anxious under pressure. Darla encouraged Richard to be casual and relaxed with Harold. She did not warn Richard of Harold's preferences, and she definitely didn't tell Richard to prepare. Darla set up a 15-minute meeting for Richard before a luncheon Harold had to attend. One hardly ever gets a second chance at a first impression, and Harold's negative first impression of Richard was due to Darla's subterfuge.

This type of bullying is very subtle. On the surface, the bully, Darla, and the target, Richard, had a good working relationship, but the bully was a sniper, using her position power to discredit him. Darla surreptitiously manipulated Richard and Harold to experience each other the way she wanted. This passive-aggressive bullying hid Darla's true feelings behind the pretext of helping a junior executive. Darla is a Belier, one who acts covertly with subtlety and without empathy or feelings of remorse.

The critical incident report explaining what happened follows.

CRITICAL INCIDENT REPORT FOR RICHARD'S STORY

Situation 1: I asked Darla to introduce me to Harold. Darla agreed to organize a meeting because she knew Harold very well. I was also having meetings with others in the company, a fact that apparently did not go down well with Darla.

Behavior 1: I have a laid-back style, and I often ramble when conversing. Harold has a cogent and concise style of conversing. Darla set up our meeting just before lunch. She knew Harold would be amenable to meeting me, but only for the 15 minutes allotted, which would not be enough time for me to convey much, given my habit of rambling. Darla did not prepare me on how to make the meeting successful, and she knew it would not go well given each of our styles. The meeting took place, and Harold's first impression of me was not positive. You don't get a second chance at a first impression. When I approached Darla for feedback, she feigned anger that I had made such a poor impression, given that she'd stuck out her neck for me.

Consequence 1: I failed to connect with Harold, and the impression I made was negative, which lowered Harold's opinion of HR. Meanwhile, Darla was feeling more secure in her position.

Note that based on the critical incident, Richard can script a meeting with Darla that addresses his suspicions but also how they need to work together in the future. Beliers pose a challenge as their motives are deeply hidden from view.

RICHARD'S SCRIPT

Richard: Darla, thank you for this meeting and for helping to arrange the meeting with Harold. I learned a valuable lesson from that experience. I neglected to realize that you are someone whom I should learn from as well. I was in too much of a hurry and didn't ask you about Harold's preferred form of communication. And I overlooked how valuable you have been and continue to be to the company. I want to know how HR can help you with your responsibilities. HR is here for you. Whatever you need, we will be responsive to those needs.

Darla: Thank you. Good to know.

Richard: One question. What should I have done for the meeting with Harold for it to have gone better?

Darla: It seems he doesn't like small talk!

Richard: You are correct. I wish I'd known that before I went into the meeting. [Pause.]

Darla: You are an adult and should have been able to figure that out.

Richard: Going forward, I would like it if you would warn me if I am approaching a person in a way that will not result in the best outcome or a productive relationship with that person. Will you give me a heads-up in the future?

Darla: Yes, sure.

A worst-case scenario for Richard could have been an angry reaction from Darla. The anger would have masked the Belier's intention of sabotage or manipulation or her attempt to be more secure in her job. Richard would have had to deal with the anger by reflecting back the emotion with a comment such as "You seem upset. Help me understand why." Then he would need to listen and attend to her. Richard needs to maintain a good relationship with Darla at work, and it is she, not Richard, who suffers from the underlying insecurities that are causing her to behave badly.

YOUR BELIER SCRIPT

What is expected:

_____

_____

_____

What is observed:

_____

_____

_____

CRITICAL INCIDENT 1

Situation:

_____

_____

_____

Behavior:

_____

_____

_____

Consequence:

_____

_____

_____

You say:

_____

_____

_____

The Belier may say:

_____

_____

_____

Your response:

_____

_____

_____

CRITICAL INCIDENT 2

Situation:

_____

_____

_____

Behavior:

_____

_____

_____

Consequence:

_____

_____

_____

You say:

_____

_____

_____

The Belier may say:

_____

_____

_____

Your response:

_____

_____

_____

Although bullies often back down when confronted, the Belier may not agree so readily at first. This is why a script is particularly effective with this kind of bully; you can have several approaches during the conversation. The conversation alone may reduce the Belier's tendency to spread false rumors. If you continue to be authentic and direct with the Belier, he will be more authentic with you. The conversation should begin the process of resetting your relationship.

Usually a Belier has reasons for her actions. It could be fear of being overlooked, feelings of inadequacy, or both. It could be that she wants the attention because she doesn't feel worthy. You can usually diagnose the source of difficulty by actively listening, empathizing, and giving full attention to the Belier. You may uncover a lack of understanding, misinformation about her intentions, feelings of jealousy and insecurity, or simply her habit of gossiping or demeaning without considering its impact on you and others. And though it is important to understand the source of the behavior and not take it personally, you need to convey clearly the inappropriate nature of the behavior.

REPUTATION MANAGEMENT

John was an attractive, intelligent advertising executive in his early forties when he learned, too late, that his reputation had soured his chances for promotion at the large digital technology company where he had been for five years. Upon joining the firm, he had been embraced by all the junior executives, mostly men, who interfaced with him on key marketing issues or worked with him on communications strategy. He called his group of colleagues the "locker room." Their motto was, "We work hard, we play hard, and we don't let the women in." Although married to a working woman whose career he fully supported, at work he hung with the guys, playing racquetball at lunch and getting beers together after work, and he was always in and out of their offices.

He had an excellent relationship with his male boss, the executive vice president, and he was convinced that he was in line for a promotion. But there was a sudden reorganization at the top of the company, and his boss was asked to take voluntary retirement. Kate, who ran global affairs, was brought in to take his boss's place. Within days, she too reorganized, and she made John's job redundant. He was offered another position in sales or the option to leave with a package. He chose the latter. When he asked human resources what he did to earn Kate's displeasure, he did not receive a specific response other than being told how important positive relationships are at work. He was able to surmise that he was perceived as preferring to be with and to work with only men. Kate had enough on her plate to deal with without having to tackle his perceived machismo.

Reputation management is more than just managing your online presence. It is taking a regular good, hard look at how you are perceived in the company by reports, peers, and superiors. This can be done by either human resources or an outside coach using a 360 stakeholder assessment tool. But there are simpler ways to gauge how you are perceived. John might have taken advantage of this before Kate arrived on the scene. We recommend the following:

- Upon taking a new job, set up meetings with your boss two weeks, six weeks, and three months in to ask how you are doing. Report on what you have accomplished and ask for feedback on your performance but also on your relationships with your coworkers and important stakeholders in your success.

- Identify your key stakeholders: those whose opinion of you and your work will have a direct impact on your success or failure. Define the kind of relationship you would like to have with each stakeholder and the steps you will take to make that happen.

- Understand that perception is reality in the eyes of those who count. If you socialize at work with only one gender, for example, you may be perceived as sexist. If you are late, you may be viewed as unreliable. If you don't speak up in meetings, you may be seen as passive. If you don't address your bully, you may be thought of as weak and as a victim.

- Meet with your key stakeholders as soon as possible and set up regular communications with them. Discuss the work you are doing and see if it is aligned with their goals and interests and the mission of the company. Check to see if they have heard anything about your performance. Ask what else you can do. Take notes on the meeting and periodically e-mail reports to them on what you are working on that might be of interest to them or articles that might be germane.

The chart in Figure 3.1 will help you diagnose and manage key stakeholder relationships.

Stakeholder Name	Current Relationship and Status	His or Her Stake in Your Success	Future Desired Relationship	Steps to a Better Relationship

FIGURE 3.1 Stakeholder Analysis Chart

SPECIFIC TIPS TO USE WHEN CONFRONTING A BELIER

- Beliers, although usually introverted, are shrewd and clever. Don't try to outsmart or out-quip them in the conversation. Don't take the bait. Be direct and stay on point. If the Belier tries to derail you, move on to your second critical incident as another example of the behavior and its impact that you are experiencing.

- Because Beliers are most likely operating out of insecurity, setting up a time to get to know them better and allowing them to get to know you can go a long way toward reassuring the Belier that you are not out to get him.

- Enlisting the Belier's help in quelling the rumors is the quickest way to reset your reputation in the company. As he was the original source of the lies, he will have credibility. If you cannot get this commitment, identify some trustworthy colleagues and tell them that you have heard these rumors and share with them the truth. Also, inform your boss as quickly as possible what you have experienced and the steps you are taking to reestablish your credibility. Ask for her help as well in quelling the rumor mill.

CHECKLIST OF THE BELIER'S BEHAVIORAL CHARACTERISTICS

☐ Changes the mood of conversation constantly from friendly to severe

☐ Demonstrates passivity one minute and aggression the next

☐ Speaks negatively about anyone not present at a meeting

☐ Is selfish and petty but tries to conceal it

☐ Orchestrates negative campaigns against the good-faith efforts of others

☐ Tries to harm targets without drawing attention to himself

☐ Misrepresents the truth to discredit and demean targets

☐ Often pretends to be supportive while discrediting targets

☐ Maliciously gossips to bring others down

☐ Slanders the character of others

☐ Is a liar and rumormonger behind the scenes

☐ Is cold in demeanor and avoids any type of authentic communication

☐ Is humorless and stubborn

☐ Has unstable relationships with others

☐ Is emotionally dishonest

☐ Engages in negative clandestine campaigns to deny a target's growth at work

☐ Causes damage to a target's career without feelings of remorse

☐ Reduces morale at work by pitting one employee against another

☐ Distorts the truth to create unnecessary drama at work

☐ Purposely creates conflict and crisis from behind the scenes

☐ Displays variability of moods that change without notice

☐ Is excessively hypercritical of others

☐ Is deceitful and scheming

☐ Manipulates others' perceptions

If you have checked eight or more of the items on this list, you are undoubtedly dealing with a Belier.

HOW TO ENGAGE THE BLOCKER

You will never reach higher ground if
you are always pushing others down.
—Jeffrey Benjamin,
Real Life Habits for Success

It is important to remember that the Blocker is most likely a perfectionist who is dealing with a lot of fear: a fear of failure and a fear of lack of control. Although his bullying may be targeted, the target should try not to take the blocking personally. Dealing with Blockers is usually best when it is immediate and in the moment because they usually do their blocking in meetings when people are trying to get things done. If allowed to block ideas as they are being shared, the Blocker will only pick up steam, and soon others will copy the behavior. When blocked in a meeting, you should come back with something along the lines of "Excuse me, I would like to finish my thought please" or "I am not quite through. I need one more minute."

Over time, if you are consistent in dealing with the Blocker in the moment or shortly after an incident, you may help her change her behavior, at least in meetings. If there is no behavior change in meetings or in conversations with you, you will need to confront the Blocker privately in a quiet place and use paraphrasing skills throughout the conversation. Paraphrasing will make the exchange of information less one-sided, and it is a style of communication in which you reveal what you understand about what the other person is saying and request more information about what you do not understand. In this way, trust may be established with the Blocker.

Typical characteristics of Blockers are the following:

- They repel any new ideas and are suspicious of those who present them, making personal connections difficult. The overall impact on others is separation and isolation rather than collaboration.

- Blockers love bringing increasing levels of detail to the process of getting work done. Yet doing that without prioritizing the details can cause work to stall because no one knows exactly what to do first.

- They are consumed by details, procedures, rules, and the planning of tasks—yet they find it hard to make decisions once all the data is collected. A decision means they have to give up control of the process. Any attempts to come up with a faster, more focused way of doing things will draw fire from the Blockers, who find disagreement or change to be disrespectful.

- If the Blocker is the boss, the employee with new ideas will be targeted and micromanaged. This may continue until the target is totally exhausted and drained of his intrinsic motivation. The Blocker continues to be negative, naysaying, nitpicky, and whiny. The negativity sucks all the positive energy from others on the team as well. Although the Blocker may not raise her voice very often, she manages to kill colleagues' enthusiasm and their desire to perform well. It only gets worse over time.

- The Blocker boss does not give praise, positive reinforcement, or financial or other incentives, but he will dispense plenty of criticism via demeaning and harassing comments.

- A Blocker boss often becomes suspect of the workers around her and their intentions and motivations. She may perceive that she is being falsely criticized. The Blocker will then go ballistic and become argumentative, hypersensitive, aggressive, and sarcastic.

- Blockers can be unforgiving of criticisms of their work or the way they get things done. They interpret criticism as attacks on their character. They suspect everyone is against them, and they become preoccupied with doubts about the loyalty and trust of others. This is when the bullying can escalate into more aggressive behavior, such as blaming or falsely accusing others, being irritable at having to listen or attend to others, and being hypertense in meetings with others. Blockers can become a source of great stress in the workplace. They exhibit impatience when working with others and have an overwhelming need to control the task.

Ted's Story

Nadine was one of the founders of a very successful e-commerce retail company and was serving as its chief operating officer. In the five years it had been in business, the company had doubled its revenues each year and had won several accolades from the business community for its fast and impressive growth. The company had also hired over 50 employees to build the brand and the digital technology that was the business engine of the enterprise.

One of the most senior hires, Ted, became increasingly concerned that the business was serving only one industry and that doing so could be problematic because of the volatility of retail sales, which could be hurt by a slow market. In a leadership meeting, Ted suggested diversifying into other areas of trade using existing technology. Nadine immediately reprimanded Ted for going offtrack, and she used an abrupt and dismissive tone of voice while stating that the company had enough on its plate and that Ted should stick to the original mission.

When Ted brought it back up in private, Nadine again rebuked him for getting ahead of himself, and she shut down the conversation. She continued to cut him off in meetings, using a harsh tone in front of others, as she deflected his ideas for alternative ways to support and protect the business. Eventually, Ted chose to go to another company. Two years later, Nadine's company dissolved, following the steep downward trajectory of the retail market. With no alternative strategy in place to offset the cyclical retail market conditions, the company had no choice but to close its doors.

Nadine, in spite of her entrepreneurial background, was a classic Blocker. The ramifications of her behavior on her and her company were disastrous and might have been avoided. She was so obsessively focused on her way of doing things, she was unable to tolerate any new or creative thinking. To make matters worse, her delivery style was degrading, impersonal, ungracious, and overly tough, probably based on her inability to share control of strategy with anyone. Ted definitely felt not only blocked but demeaned, both privately and publicly.

Before confronting the Blocker, Ted should have prepared. He should have documented several critical incidents using the Critical Incident Technique (CIT),[1] and he should have written down what he expected when he signed on with the company and what he observed was the reality on the job.

CRITICAL INCIDENT REPORT FOR TED'S STORY

Situation 1: This is a company founded on the basis of a creative idea. It is presumably a workplace where innovative thinking is appreciated. I joined with the expectations that I could contribute to its growth and well-being and also look to ways to expand the business model. My loyalty and commitment to the company are strong, and I have enormous enthusiasm for my job.

Behavior 1: When I gathered enough intelligence to raise a concern about our lack of diversification, I was treated like a child by Nadine and rebuked in front of the whole leadership team. Also, I observed that every time, subsequent to that meeting, that I raised an idea or made a suggestion, I was cut off and my comment dismissed. Using a harsh tone of voice, she continuously rejected any suggestions or comments I made either in private or publicly in meetings.

Consequence 1: I felt unappreciated. I felt like I was wasting everyone's time. After several failed attempts to discuss this situation and behavior, I realized that she would never listen. By no means my first choice, I felt that I had to look elsewhere for employment.

TED'S SCRIPT

Ted should arrange the meeting in a private office and, one hopes, at a time when Nadine is less stressed.

> *Ted:* Nadine, in a very short period of time, I have come to love this company, and I hope to have a long and successful career here. By nature, I am also very protective of the company for which I work. It is with that deep sense of loyalty to you and the company that I raised my concern for our future in the last leadership meeting. [By preparing this delicate conversation with a statement of loyalty, Ted will seem less threatening and put the Blocker at ease that he is not quitting.] When I joined the company, I was impressed by its success and told that it was an innovative culture that had respect and tolerance for new ideas. I am surprised to have experienced the opposite when I offered suggestions for change. [Ted has now stated what he expected and then observed. He should pause and wait to see how the Blocker responds.]

Nadine: Ted, if you are referring to our last leadership meeting when I changed the subject from your idea for diversification back to our leadership agenda, you were offtrack and derailing the meeting agenda. [Nadine again dismisses Ted's concern.]

Ted: Nadine, I believe the way you handled that indicated not only your lack of respect for me, given your tone and words, but also your lack of interest in hearing that I may have detected a serious chink in our armor.

Nadine: Of course I am interested in what you have to say, but perhaps the leadership meeting was not the best place to say it. [Ted may have to concede here that he should have presented his concern to Nadine privately.]

Ted: That is a fair point, but I brought it up to you again in private and received the same response. May I know how and where you would like new ideas presented? [Ted stays on point, but he asks for clarity on the right approach to present new ideas.]

Nadine: Ted, I had no intention to upset you. It is a tense time for the company. I don't want to suppress your ideas. Let's discuss how we might revisit your concerns and determine the next steps.

Ted: I can understand that this has been a rough quarter and that it has been stressful. [Paraphrasing back what he understands about the other person's comments is a great technique for defusing any residual anger in the Blocker.] As I said, I like working here, and I only want the best for you and the company's future. How about we set a meeting after the next earnings call to go over my thoughts about protecting that future? [Ted establishes a next step for the two of them.]

What is apparent in this story is that Ted wasn't paying attention to all the factors that might have provoked Nadine to treat him poorly. Likewise, Nadine was unaware of the strength of her tone of voice and may be more careful in the future. Her bullying might have been due to the stress, more likely the fear, that she was feeling at work, so time will tell whether this work relationship can be remediated. At least, Ted will feel better that he addressed it with Nadine.

John's Story

John was the vice president of communications and marketing of a medium-sized full-service advertising firm. He was viewed as a real talent in his field, repeatedly creating innovative and cutting-edge marketing ideas for the company's clients. The CEO, Tim, brought him into all the client meetings in which new strategic thinking was on the agenda because he knew he could rely on John not only to think on his feet but also to present ideas that would address the clients' needs in a coherent and enthusiastic way.

However, John's direct boss, Eric, the COO, was not as pleased with John's growing reputation as an up-and-coming star in the firm. John's increasingly close relationship with the CEO made Eric worry about his own future. He became more irritable and paranoid. Eric's value to the company was as a master of all the details of operations, and he insisted on absolute control of the process. All his direct reports always followed up with Eric and never went to the CEO as John sometimes did. Eric also felt that he had the best ideas for the company.

So Eric the Blocker took action. Eric dismissively blocked any ideas John put forward and continuously referred to his youth and inexperience, always explaining the "right" way to do something whenever John made a suggestion in meetings. John's enthusiasm and energy eventually dissipated, and he left the company.

John's ideas and suggestions were rejected by his boss, Eric, continuously until, dejected, he moved to another company. Had John had the tools to meet and discuss his disappointment with Eric, there might have been a different outcome.

Blockers bully directly by preventing any significant input from others. They do this to ensure that the work is completed "correctly"—that is, their way. That can happen only if they are in control. They often exhibit obsessive-compulsive behavior, and they have perfectionist tendencies. If they don't get their way, they become paranoid. Even though the Blocker may not intend to harm another's productivity, his belief that only if *he* controls the way the work is done will it be done right *is* bullying. Blockers' comments are often blunt and seemingly negative, but those comments are based more on their own fears of failure. They do not show any generosity during interpersonal interactions, and they are obsessed with controlling, withholding, and limiting information in an exchange with others in order to feel more in control.

John should have set up a meeting with Eric. Before doing so, he should have documented at least one critical incident.

CRITICAL INCIDENT REPORT
FOR JOHN'S STORY

Situation 1: Our team meeting is a time when all of us expect a chance to share our ideas and leverage our expertise with others. Eric, apparently as a result of his seniority and position power, feels free to interrupt almost every suggestion I or others make, bringing the conversation back to what we "should" do and not "what is possible" to do.

Behavior 1: Every single time I offer my thoughts and ideas, Eric swoops in, even before I have finished my sentence, with comments such as "That is not right," "Someone with more experience wouldn't say that," "That is how a young person would see it," and concluding with, "We are definitely not doing it that way."

Consequence 1: As a result, I have been more and more hesitant to offer any comments at these meetings. I notice others doing the same. My perception is that the full talent of the team is not being tapped. Moreover, I feel we can't be open at these meetings and that we are misusing our time together. The company is losing the potential of collaborative problem solving and decision-making. I do not feel that I am adding value.

One of the essential elements in John's discussion with Eric is to help him understand the unproductive way meetings are run and the impact of Eric's behavior on him and the team.

JOHN'S SCRIPT

John: Thanks for agreeing to talk with me. Since we have so many meetings together, I wanted to share my thoughts on how to capitalize on both our past experiences. I can learn so much from you and already have. Likewise, I expected to contribute and participate in the team's strategic thinking from my own experience. But I observed that you feel your way of doing things is the best way to do it. Am I wrong in that perception?

Eric: I do feel I have more experience than anyone on the team.

John: Have you thought about how the team might feel about always being told what to do?

Eric: No. I don't believe feelings should play a role in business. [Remember, Blockers are preoccupied with order and control, deny their own emotions, and lack the ability to see other people's emotions.]

John: Well, let me share with you the way I see it. [John shouldn't ask for permission because Eric may not give it.] I believe I have something to contribute to these meetings, and I feel I am being blocked from sharing my input.

Eric: Are you sure you have something to contribute? I haven't heard much.

John: Well, yes, I do have a lot to contribute, but you have prevented me from talking at meetings.

Eric: Perhaps your real issue is with my being so knowledge-able.

John: [Ignoring that comment and using paraphrasing.] Your thoroughness and focus for near-perfect outcomes is good and will help all of us achieve success. I understand what you have accomplished on project A. However, I'm not sure I understand other people's take on how project A connects with project B, for which Mark and I have responsibility. I believe others would be better served by my perceptions and thoughts if I could offer them at our meetings. They too might have good insights that could be helpful. [John would use his critical incident document at this point in the conversation.] Will you permit me and others to speak more at our meetings? I believe everyone on the team would then feel much more involved.

Eric: I think it will be a waste of time.

John: I'm disappointed you think that. I hope you can agree on one change. Can we have the first 10 uninterrupted minutes at our weekly hour-and-a-half meetings to share our work and suggestions with you? And might those reports come before you speak, so you can hear and reflect on our ideas?

Eric: OK. I'll try it once, but if it doesn't provide value, we will run the meetings my way. [This is a step in the right direction. John now needs to prepare the team so that the time will be well spent.]

YOUR BLOCKER SCRIPT

What is expected:

_____

_____

_____

What is observed:

_____

_____

_____

CRITICAL INCIDENT 1

Situation:

_____

_____

_____

Behavior:

_____

_____

_____

Consequence:

_____

_____

_____

You say:

_____

_____

_____

The Blocker may say:

_____

_____

_____

Your response:

_____

_____

_____

Critical Incident 2

Situation:

_____

_____

_____

Behavior:

_____

_____

_____

Consequence:

_____

_____

_____

You say:

_____

_____

_____

The Blocker may say:

_____

_____

_____

Your response:

_____

_____

_____

Blockers must learn that their actions shut down others and prevent them from offering their thoughts and insights on the work at hand. They must understand that their attempts to control every idea or action results in a lack of openness because of their insistence that others comply and submit exactly to their way of doing things. This, in fact, will drive out very creative and ambitious people, especially millennials, who are known to have little tolerance for oppressive management.

Within a team setting, Blockers must learn that listening skills, an empathic perspective, and the ability to be attentive will encourage team members to do their best work. They must also be made aware that their obsessive-compulsive behavior results not only in dismissing other people's ideas but also in dismissing the people themselves. Blockers need to understand the value of having various members of the group collaborate and contribute to the team's achievements—and that doing so will get the Blockers closer to their goal of perfection.

Most important, Blockers need to appreciate that no one will ever do the job exactly as they would. A different end result, however, could be even better and serve as a testament to their leadership. A manager might remind the entire team every so often that all of their contributions allow for a better result. Some teams use ground rules, posted on a flip chart or a permanent sign on the wall, that prompt the team to listen to everyone's complete ideas without interrupting or judging the merit of those ideas until people have had a chance to finish.

We have seen teams elect an *evaluator* before the beginning of a meeting. In addition to participating, the evaluator guides the team members to being better collaborators and more inclusive of all ideas as well as making more effective decisions. According to one popular ground rule for such a plan, there are two phases of successful collaboration efforts. The first phase is to encourage idea generation by not making early judgments so that all ideas are received and considered with equal weight. The second phase is to then judge and evaluate those ideas.

With Blockers, your aim is to keep them comfortable in continuous communication. Learn what they know and make every effort to show them what you know, but not in a competitive way. You need to understand their world view so that they are comfortable with you and trust you. Ideally, their desire to protect their own way of doing things will lessen over time, resulting in a more open exchange of information.

SPECIFIC TIPS TO USE WHEN CONFRONTING A BLOCKER

- A Blocker often acts out of fear of a loss of control, to the point of obsession. Do research, if you can, on what factors may be contributing to the Blocker's sensitivity about being in control. Was there a prior incident during her watch for which she was punished or reprimanded? Is she going through a personal situation that is causing stress? Are there other stress factors? This may affect both your understanding of what she is dealing with and the timing of your confrontation.

- If you are dealing with a Blocker, be sure not to present too many ideas at once. Because of his need to control information, logistics, and operations, he may be able to hear only one idea at a time. Speak slowly and carefully to ensure that he really hears the idea.

- Blockers are often blunt and harsh in their delivery. This is partly how they have built up their power in the company—by being difficult. People will avoid them, leaving them to control even more. As Blockers may never have received feedback on their tone, you may help them understand its impact by describing how it makes you feel.

- Consider sharing your ideas with other influential members of the team and ask that they support you when you present it. Getting their feedback and insight will also help you refine the idea.

- Blockers present a dilemma to their companies. They do excellent work, control a lot of important and strategic information, and usually aren't going anywhere. However, if the Blocker is preventing your growth and advancement and discussions have not helped, it may be time to address the problem with human resources or with the Blocker's boss. Your documentation of the critical incidents will be very valuable in this meeting.

CHECKLIST OF THE BLOCKER'S BEHAVIORAL CHARACTERISTICS

☐ Blocks progress by rejecting all ideas and arguing too much

☐ Seeks sympathy for her monumental effort to get things right

☐ Controls all aspects of a project in an obsessive-compulsive way

☐ Monopolizes control of information, logistics, and operations

☐ Prevents openness, efficiency, and collaboration at work

☐ Has a pervasive preoccupation with orderliness and perfection

☐ Focuses on mental and interpersonal control of targets

☐ Compulsively focuses on controlling tasks at work

☐ Controls and restricts his emotions and the emotions of others

☐ Discourages, dissuades, and denies targets from contributing their ideas

☐ Obsessively focuses on keeping her targets working the way she works

☐ Overemphasizes details, rules, standards, and schedules

☐ Overanalyzes to the point of paralysis

☐ Lacks a humanistic, encouraging, and affiliative interpersonal style at work

☐ Tends to target those with a lot of ideas or with suggestions to streamline work

☐ Targets those who want to divide up the work

☐ Brings more and more detail into a process

☐ Perceives as threats those who have a highly intrinsic motivation to do well

☐ Punishes with negative, naysaying, nitpicky, and whiny comments

☐ Kills a target's desire to do well on her own

☐ Never praises or gives positive reinforcement

☐ Criticizes with demeaning and harassing comments

☐ Is blunt and critical

If you have checked eight or more of the items on this list, you are undoubtedly dealing with a Blocker.

HOW TO ENGAGE
THE BRAGGART

None are so empty as those who are full of themselves.
—Benjamin Whichot

Braggarts perceive themselves in an idealized way. They imagine others see them in the same way, and they are usually not aware, or capable of understanding, that their narcissism, boasting, and retaliatory behavior are received as bullying. If the Braggart is an extreme narcissist, it may be very difficult to intervene, but by becoming familiar with a Braggart's dynamic, which is usually repetitive, you can adroitly interrupt him during his one-way communication to redirect the conversation to a more collaborative one. Consider the answers to these questions before your meeting with the Braggart:

- How does any conversation begin? Does it immediately turn to a self-indulgent story about something that happened to the Braggart?

- Does the Braggart ever ask you about yourself or your work?

- Does one story usually lead to another story?

- If you try to share a similar story, does she try to one-up you with a better story?

- Does the Braggart elaborate with unnecessary detail and exaggeration to create more drama?

- Do you feel exhausted after he has finished? Have you given him your full attention, hoping to get into the conversation, only to find out that he will not permit you to speak?

- Are these conversations draining your productivity to the point that you want to avoid the Braggart in the hallway or elevator?

The Braggart has a self-important "I" that pushes out others, and the result is an empathetic deficit and unremorseful posture. The Braggart feels the need to feed her overinflated sense of self regularly. Like a drug addict, the more the self-important "I" is fed, the more it needs to be fed. The Braggart will idealize her sense of self-importance, and it becomes the only mode for interacting with others. A Braggart can deflate a workplace or a team and cause a toxic environment.

To have a more productive exchange with the Braggart, remember that if you are introverted, you must become an ambivert (flexible enough to know when to listen or to talk, not overly expressive or withdrawn, and comfortable being adaptable and just a bit more extroverted). You have to *talk with* Braggarts, *not at* them, because they are very protective of their feelings of self-importance. The prearranged meeting should be one-on-one and away from any potential audience. The skill of redirection is essential. When they change the subject to make the conversation about themselves, pause for up to five seconds, acknowledge the story, and then redirect the conversation back to the task at hand. Eventually, Braggarts may recognize that you are simply trying to focus the meeting.

We have all been in meetings in which a Braggart uses 80 percent of the time talking about himself, usually in a charming way. There is nothing wrong with a charming delivery, but if it is at the exclusion of others, you are dealing with a Braggart. Meetings—whether one-on-one or for an entire team—are for each individual involved to contribute to the ongoing work. That can't happen if one person is always holding court and suppressing discussion because of his unhealthy need to be admired.

You will recognize Braggarts by the following characteristics:

- They live with an idealized sense of grandness about their ability to lead, to succeed, and to be the smartest people in the room.

- They portray themselves as unique such that only very intelligent people can understand them, yet they want and need the admiration and compliance of everyone.

- They see others as their props or audience members in their monologues.

- They brag because it feeds their need to feel worthy when they actually may feel unworthy. The bragging is designed to make them feel as if they have consequence and standing.

- They discriminate against others for their beliefs, age, size, looks, gender, ethnicity, and country of origin. They are often unable and unwilling to see someone else's point of view, much less how the other person might feel about something.

- They never allow others to contribute in a meaningful way to discussions or any work projects.

- They can be exploitive of others with talent, especially those whom they envy. They will try to utilize the talent of others for their own benefit.

- They have an empathy deficit, and they do not want to deal with the feelings of others. Yet they are very sensitive to comments about them that come close to a slight or criticism, and they respond with aggressive anger and insults.

- They do not recognize the psychological or emotional harm that they cause, and they show no signs of remorse when the target shows frustration, upset, or other signs of stress. In fact, once the Braggart draws an emotional response from the target, the Braggart will see the target as weak.

- If in a position of power, the Braggart's boasting can initially cause him to look very wise, whereas everyone else is a listener in his audience. The Braggart steals the life from a one-on-one conversation by keeping the focus on himself, his exaggerated accomplishments, his fantasies about his own experience, and his insistence that he is brilliant, with special knowledge and gifts. In a meeting, he will talk and talk until the time is up, at which point, he will move on to another meeting and talk about himself—again.

- They are charismatic, which increases our trust in them and lowers our defense mechanisms. Remember, though, it is a mask that can shield a vicious authoritarian mindset.

- If you do good work for a Braggart, don't expect to be acknowledged. She will take credit for your work and display it as her own. Ironically, if employees or targets make a mistake, they can expect a double-barrel berating in which all their limitations will be aired, usually in public.

- The Braggart expects you to give him good ideas, for which he will not be grateful. If the ideas are good, he will claim them. If the ideas are bad, he will blame you.

- The social value of fairness and boundaries is very difficult for the Braggart to comprehend. A Braggart boss will expect an employee, especially one who appears vulnerable, to keep long hours at work and always comply. This boss will judge that person as unworthy or unfit for the job if the target shows tension and frustration about the work.

- An extreme Braggart will violate personal boundaries. She will start with verbal barrages of insulting commentary, challenging your competence, honesty, and value.

- Most male Braggarts expect adoration from women, and they often touch, hug, or leave their hand or arm on the woman with whom they are conversing; this unwanted physical contact is a way to affirm their own sense of self-importance. This is power positioning; the man is claiming dominance over a woman in the workplace. We train people on how to treat us by what we tolerate. If the target acquiesces and doesn't draw the boundaries, the behavior will be reinforced and will only get worse.

- They will not accept differences of opinion. They are driven to come out of any challenge as the winner even if it means lying, cheating, or stealing others' ideas.

- The Braggart is indifferent to a toxic workplace that is caused by her own self-indulgence.

- The Braggart makes it difficult to get things done. He points out problems with others who do not fit in when, in reality, the Braggart resents their competence and intelligence.

- Braggarts may manage up well in that they may be able to feign empathy to satisfy those more highly ranked in the organization, but they show a different face when they manage down.

Diana's Story

Ethan was a very large man, 6 feet, 4 inches, hefty but not fat, with a loud booming voice. When he entered the room, everyone took notice. He used his size and voice to quickly take over any conversation. His area of expertise was marketing.

He had a successful career helping to launch several companies with cutting-edge marketing strategies. He had an idea a minute, and he could never stop talking about his career wins and his ideas for the company.

Diana reported directly to Ethan, and although happy to learn from an old pro, she was growing tired of hearing the same stories from him. Also, he was full of new ideas for the future. He thought up and fleshed out the ideas alone, with no input from others. There was no room for anyone else to participate in setting the marketing strategy for the company. Ethan was basically a nice man, but by declaring himself the only innovative thinker in the company, he was indirectly demeaning Diana and others on the team. It was very difficult to interrupt him, and if you presented an idea on paper, he claimed it as his own if he liked it and dismissed it if he didn't.

His total self-absorption prevented him from sensing the significant shadow he was casting on the department's energy and morale. Diana felt at times that his monopoly of airtime, his braggadocio, and his inability to offer praise to anyone but himself might be a cover-up for a deep psychological wound he had suffered earlier on. She was even more apprehensive about confronting him.

What Diana expected in her work with Ethan was not only to learn from him but to contribute her ideas for the marketing strategy that might be different from his but equally valuable. What she observed was that Ethan had no interest in listening, questioning, or trying anything he had not created. Diana began feeling more and more like a slave to his ego.

Diana began to prepare for a meeting with Ethan during which she planned to share with him her deep disappointment in her job. She prepared by documenting her critical incidents.[1]

CRITICAL INCIDENT REPORT FOR DIANA'S STORY

Situation 1: Ethan recruited me and several of my reports to the company with the promise of an experience designing and executing new and out-of-the-box marketing campaigns. These would include developing auxiliary products in support of the main objectives of the company. Ethan talked nonstop about himself and his past accomplishments in the interviews, but I wrote it off as his trying his best to recruit me to his team. I did not expect it to be more than that.

Behavior 1: The talking and bragging continued after I joined the company. I was kept so busy implementing Ethan's ideas that I had no opportunities to create some of my own strategies. When I brought up a new idea at one of the marketing department meetings, Ethan dismissed it and told yet another story about one of his strategies that had paid off for him in the past.

Consequence 1: I noticed my enthusiasm for my job began to wane. My energy was sapped by Ethan's constant talking and storytelling. I increasingly felt like less of a contributor, and my self-esteem was quickly evaporating.

With her critical incident document in hand, Diana set up a private meeting with Ethan.

DIANA'S SCRIPT

Diana: Ethan, I set up this meeting to discuss with you something very important. When you recruited me here, it was my greatest wish that I could learn from you, which I have. I also brought 15 years of my own experience, which I thought would have value to you and the company. I expected to use my creativity on the job. I have observed that you are not interested in my creative ideas but rather just in my executing yours. As a result, I am not learning or growing as a marketing professional. I enjoy hearing your stories, but they are less helpful to me in my career at this point. If everything has to be done by you and credited to you, then I don't see a future here for me.

Ethan: I am surprised, even shocked, by this, Diana, because in all my years, I have designed award-winning campaigns and created new products that have enhanced our company's image and success . . . [This is the time for Diana to interrupt with paraphrasing and to redirect the conversation back to the real topic.]

Diana: [In an assertive voice.] We all admire and respect you, but we too need to feel like we are contributing. For example, the other day I made a suggestion that you picked up on, but then you started to tell stories about a related topic. The team was again forced to sit there and listen to stories that we had heard many times before. I am wondering if we could all participate more in the brainstorming of ideas. Perhaps we could allocate the first 30 minutes of each meeting to the team so that we can present our latest thinking on our projects. [Diana should be very specific with the Braggart about what she wants. Success will come in spurts, not all at once.] I know you do not want to sap the energy of the team. This would be a way for us all to contribute to the marketing strategy. Could we try this?

Ethan: If the team is feeling insecure, then they need to grow up. This is ridiculous.

Diana: Ethan, if the team and I don't feel we are contributing, then you may not get the best from us. [Diana shouldn't threaten Ethan but give him a clear understanding that his actions have consequences.] Let's try this out and see what happens. You may be surprised.

WAYS TO REDIRECT A BRAGGART AT A MEETING

A Braggart is likely to be a narcissist who is deeply sensitive about how he is perceived. However, if he is dominating meetings with stories of his successes and achievements, it is possible to interrupt his flow. When there is a natural break in his monologue, consider saying or doing the following:

- "I love this story. It has been very helpful to me with my customers. I used it the other day when I had a meeting with X. He had some questions, which I would appreciate hearing how you and the group would respond to . . ." [Don't stop!]

- "Martha, you were telling me something that happened to you last week that might be relevant here." [Turn to Martha and ask her to relate her story. Best to forewarn her so she can step in.]

- Stand up and go to the flip chart to create a diversion and outline the steps the Braggart took in his story, and ask for the group to consider what was going on. [Get a group conversation going.] If you are the leader at a team meeting that a Braggart is attending, you will want to set a tone of inclusion for the entire group. You might say, "All of you contribute to our success. It is always helpful to me to hear from all the members of the team. Let's have each person share his or her perspective in our discussion today."

If you set the tone at the beginning of the meeting, it is easier to interject if the Braggart begins to grandstand, gently reminding him that today, the meeting is focused on gathering everyone's ideas. Braggarts, at their core, are narcissists, fear rejection, and want to be included, but they have never been taught boundaries. They have gotten into the habit of expressing their own grandiosity and expecting adoration from others, and they dislike being audience members. They do not feel included on a team in which everybody shines. Using redirection and paraphrasing will help make Braggarts feel heard and appreciated, which will go a long way toward reducing their insecurities.

The story about Joseph and Philip that follows is a classic Braggart story. The protagonist in the critical incident and the script is the chief operations officer, Joseph, who was recently honored for his long service to the company.

Joseph's Story

Joseph had been the chief operations officer for his company for a long time, and Philip had been the company's CEO for 20 years, ever since he was hired at the very young age of 30. Philip was tall and good-looking, he appeared older than he was, and he had a booming authoritative voice. The first 10 years went well; Philip was very good at his job, and as time went on, he became even better.

But then something happened. Philip not only had to be the best-looking one at the company—he spent an inordinate amount of time fixing his hair so not a strand was out of place—but he also started peppering his conversations with stories of his exploits, intelligence, and relationships with people in high circles of society. His ego was insatiable: the more praise and deference he got, the more he needed. He started calling employees stupid in front of coworkers, interrupting them, and filling conversations with banal stories of his success. He patronized women as the weaker sex, putting his arm around them while making condescending comments like "It is all right, you will understand eventually." He even had a mural painted on the walls outside his office of all his accomplishments at the company.

He refused feedback or any input that challenged his ideas. No one on his executive team was able to talk about real problems in the company because the conversation had to be about Philip. Ultimately, many talented people left the company because of Philip's oversized sense of self. At Joseph's anniversary party, Philip made it all about himself.

CRITICAL INCIDENT REPORT FOR JOSEPH'S STORY

Situation 1: Philip was perceived as a megalomaniac, almost to the point of being tyrannical. He needed constant praise and admiration. He patronized everyone, especially women. He felt he was the smartest person in the room, and he posted all of his accomplishments over time on the wall to the right of his office so that everyone could see them as he or she sat in the waiting area. He refused to hear feedback from anyone, and he browbeat his board to go along with any plan he wanted. Over time, when you counted the number of high-caliber individuals who had left the company and the board, you would have to conclude that it was a tremendous waste of talent and money.

Behavior 1: After tolerating Philip's behavior for a long time, I had a terrible experience at my anniversary party over which Philip presided as the master of ceremonies. Philip made the party all about him, telling stories that clearly demonstrated that I was just an appendage to the CEO. This was especially hurtful given that I had masterminded a marketing campaign that had established the company's brand. After neglecting to say anything about my greatest accomplishment, Philip had everyone's attention and was not about to let it go. Philip just could not let me have my day in the sun. Philip spoke for over an hour about himself, after which everyone left.

Consequence 1: Philip crushed the event with his oppressive and toxic narcissism. I was well respected and admired in the company, but I was left with the idea that Philip had engineered the whole event to make sure he would be regarded with higher esteem than I was. People in the audience wanted to scream because it was so obvious that jealousy and insecurity prevailed that day. Philip prevented everyone in the company from feeling good about my accomplishments and bringing that feeling back to their work. Instead, they slumped back into their roles with little optimism or energy to excel. I determined that I had to address Philip's dearth of leadership skills and narcissistic ways in person.

JOSEPH'S SCRIPT

Here is a sample script showing how Joseph can address the Braggart's self-centeredness:

> *Joseph:* Thank you for agreeing to meet with me. [After some small talk.] Philip, I wanted to talk to you about the party itself. I expected to feel great about what I have accomplished for the company, but instead, I observed that you spent about 85 percent of the time talking about everything *but* my accomplishments. I think people were upset by this. What was going on?
>
> *Philip:* Your accomplishments were listed on the brochure. People could read it if they wanted. People enjoy my stories.
>
> *Joseph:* Yes, and most of what you talked about were your stories—not mine. In fact, it sounded like the party was dedicated to your accomplishments.
>
> *Philip:* Well, I am their CEO.
>
> *Joseph:* Yes, you are their leader, but leadership is not about you. It is about them. Philip, when you dominate my party or any

other conversation with personal stories that don't always apply to work, people either lose their energy, become uninterested, or are frankly bored with your self-commentary. It seems you don't value them or their experience.

Philip: I am just trying to pass on to the group what I have learned.

Joseph: A relevant story is good, but you should also hear what others have to contribute and allocate time for that. They all want to do well.

Philip: It's not my fault that some people don't talk or don't want to talk. I am good at talking, not listening.

Joseph: It is good you know that. You might want to cultivate listening skills in your remaining years as CEO. If you are interested, I have a good book you may want to read on this subject. It is important to acknowledge everyone's contributions and achievements at celebrations like mine. It is highly motivating, and it shows that you respect everyone's hard work. Please think about what I've said today. We can pick up the discussion another time.

A worst-case scenario might be as follows:

Philip: It's not my fault some people don't talk or don't want to talk. I am good at talking, not listening. I am the boss, and I will do it my way. Your experience should not eclipse my leadership in the present. They are followers. You are a follower. I am the leader.

Joseph: You are the leader, and as the leader, it is important to acknowledge everyone's contributions and achievements at celebrations like mine. It is highly motivating and shows that you respect everyone's hard work. Showing them that your leadership is the focal point at all meetings is your choice. It is sad and demotivating that you see it that way. Please think about it. We can pick up the discussion another time.

YOUR BRAGGART SCRIPT

What is expected:

_____

_____

_____

What is observed:

_____

_____

_____

CRITICAL INCIDENT 1

Situation:

_____

_____

_____

Behavior:

_____

_____

_____

Consequence:

_____

_____

_____

You say:

_____

_____

_____

The Braggart may say:

_____

_____

_____

Your response:

_____

_____

_____

CRITICAL INCIDENT 2

Situation:

_____

_____

_____

Behavior:

_____

_____

_____

Consequence:

_____

_____

_____

You say:

_____

_____

_____

The Braggart may say:

_____

_____

_____

Your response:

_____

_____

_____

SPECIFIC TIPS TO USE WHEN CONFRONTING A BRAGGART

- Braggarts love an audience, so confronting a Braggart is usually best done in a private meeting.

- Braggarts can be decent people underneath their self-absorbed need for social approval. Gently appeal to their common sense and their desire to do well.

- Braggarts may not have received a lot of constructive feedback. It is important that you are clear and honest when you share with her your experiences with her and their effect on your and others' performance.

- If you are an introvert, be an ambivert when dealing with a Braggart. That means you will use more energy in the conversation and be less passive.

- If you are an extrovert, you may need to slow down the exchange a bit. That means being very mindful of what he is saying and how you are responding.

- If it seems that you are getting nowhere when dealing with a Braggart, you may be making more progress than she lets on.

- Remember to talk *with* Braggarts—not *at* them.

CHECKLIST OF THE BRAGGART'S BEHAVIORAL CHARACTERISTICS

☐ Seeks recognition by excessive bragging about himself

☐ Closes down conversation by turning every topic back to herself

☐ Uses discriminating language that divides people according to their differences

☐ Oppressively rolls over others in conversation

☐ Declares self-importance by demeaning everyone else's efforts

☐ Has an inflated self-image as a result of self-absorption and self-adoration

☐ Abrasively inserts, asserts, intrudes, dictates, and declares self-importance

☐ Has an empathy deficit and unremorseful disposition

☐ Portrays self as unique, special, and grand

☐ Is unwilling to allow others to talk unless it supports his views

☐ Never gives credit and steals others' credit if they are successful

☐ Whenever attention is fixed by someone else, refocuses it back to self

☐ Has no sense of fairness or sharing with others on the team

☐ Has poor listening and attending skills

☐ Excessively teases and talks over others

☐ Hates hearing of others' successes, especially those of targets

☐ Insults others with barrages of demeaning statements

☐ Has to win even if she has to lie, cheat, and steal ideas from others

☐ Uses verbal monologues that discredit others and intimidate targets

☐ Prevents work from getting done by pointing to problems with people

☐ Is preoccupied with vanity, prestige, and power

☐ Exaggerates her talent and achievements

☐ Expects constant praise and admiration

☐ Is unable to apologize

☐ Expects others to go along with him no matter what

☐ Fails to recognize people's emotions, needs, and wants

☐ Is jealous of others and believes others are jealous of her

☐ Feels hurt when slighted but can't see his own rejection of others

☐ Has fragile self-esteem

☐ Uses dramatic poses and wears noticeable clothing to draw attention

If you have checked eight or more of the items on this checklist, you are undoubtedly dealing with a Braggart.

HOW TO ENGAGE THE BRUTE

Leadership at one time meant muscle;
but today it means getting along with people.
—Mahatma Gandhi

Daniel had just hopped onto the treadmill at the gym for his daily 40-minute routine. Listening to CNN on his earphones, he reacted with surprise to an angry-looking man who tapped him hard on the shoulder and aggressively said, "When are you getting off this machine?" Daniel, who could make out only part of the question, removed his earphones and asked the man to repeat what he'd said. He did so with even more emotion. Daniel answered, "I just got on." The man retorted, "I need to know when you are getting off so I can plan my workout schedule!"

This is a classic example of an insensitive Brute with an anger-management issue. His total lack of self-discipline and control over his emotions caused him to be oblivious to Daniel's situation (earphones and in the zone). The gym was not crowded; three quarters of the machines were empty. Yet he impulsively demanded to know then and there when he could use the treadmill. The way he approached Daniel indicated an inability to have a civil dialogue. It is in these instances when a Brute needs immediate feedback about the impact he is having on you. Daniel responded clearly and strongly, "Sir, I just got on the machine, and you have some nerve using that tone of voice with me." The man stomped off.

Would we all be able to handle Brutes adroitly like this in the workplace? Daniel stayed calm in tone and voice, and he made it clear that he wasn't going to engage with this man. Importantly, Daniel nipped the interaction in the bud. This is what we need to do in the workplace. Brute bullies need to be stopped in the moment.

Brutes are especially difficult to deal with because of their potentially explosive reaction to being confronted. We have found that most people fear their dealings with Brutes more than the three other types of bullies. In fact, many of us find it very challenging to look at a person acting irrationally in the eye and tell her she is being a bully, but we need to rise to the challenge. When the Brute is aggressive, competitive, and confrontational, you need to stay calm, use a firm voice, and work through the discussion patiently. Most important, you must remember not to take it personally! The rage that boils up in a Brute quickly is most likely rooted in her psyche from trauma that occurred years ago. You have unwittingly stimulated it, but—though it is always helpful to review your own actions and engagements before the event—you are not to blame for the Brute's behavior.

To create distance and the ability to depersonalize your interactions with the Brute, it is helpful to answer the following questions:

- When and how often does the Brute bully?

- Where does he bully? Are there obvious triggers that set him off?

- Has the Brute ever admitted that she has been a bully?

- Does he bully peers and subordinates only? What about superiors? How does he behave around them?

- How does the Brute bully? Is it tone of voice, language, derogatory gestures, or the more threatening use of her body?

- Is he lacking empathy?

- Does she exhibit remorse after she explodes?

- Is the Brute disrespectful to all authority except his own?

With answers to these questions, you have some facts at your disposal. They will show you that this behavior is not about you, and they will give you some insight into why she is a Brute. You will be mentally prepared to address her behavior by documenting the critical incidents and building a script with carefully crafted and ready-made lines to use in the encounter that will allow you to remain emotionally poised and composed should an attack occur.

Brutes can be identified easily by the following:

- Brutes will break promises to coworkers and employees just for the thrill of it and because they can. Brutes have not developed the skill of empathy, and that prevents them from realizing the harm they cause or from observing proper interpersonal interactions and personal boundaries.

- The Brutes' rules are to be obeyed over and above any standards set forth by the company. They force others to break the rules, and if subordinates refuse, they berate them for disobeying. If the targets, or any employees under their control, violate the Brutes' rules, they will be labeled as weak and not yet promotable or capable of handling greater responsibilities at work.

- Brutes usually pick on their targets' gender, ethnic background, age, sexual orientation, level in the organization, tenure, or, if they have them, insecurities or personal sensitivities. If the targets get out of line, expect consistent public humiliation via verbal comments and threats that belittle and diminish them.

- Brutes are loud and visible; they are the easiest type of bullies to identify. Their emotional rants can escalate to the point of absurdity. (One executive we coached would get so worked up when his ideas were challenged that he would yell with spit coming out of his mouth.)

- Brutes impulsively roll over others, crushing their aspirations and goals without consideration of the consequences.

- Brutes do not recognize the rights of others, such as personal space, freedom of expression, and career growth. They violate the rights of others regularly.

- Brutes care little about safety or the psychological or emotional health of others. They put others in harm's way without consideration or sensitivity. If anything harmful happens—physically, psychologically, or emotionally—to the targets or other bystanders, they feel no remorse.

- Brutes will break interpersonal norms of propriety by using crude language to shock others at work. If others do not follow suit, they become targets because they are seen as weak. Those who dare to disagree with the Brutes will suffer abuse until they are driven out of the organization.

- The range of bullying behaviors expressed by Brutes begins with antiteam behaviors to divide and conquer employees. The intimidating, yelling, harassing, discriminating, and defaming of character through slander, publicly attacking employees for not performing well, threatening loss of a job, engaging in inappropriate sexually based interactions, using physically demonstrative body language that implies dominance, emoting with volatility, pouting, throwing temper tantrums, and physically assaulting others are all part of the Brutes' tool kit. Extreme cases can become violent.

- Brutes abuse their power with consistent verbal and written barrages of reprimands, accusing others of instability, insobriety, dishonesty, and other forms of personal condemnation.

- Brutes can't disagree without becoming completely disagreeable.

- Brutes are witty, intelligent, and charming in interviews and ironically garner promotions and raises in the workplace. But they are soon unmasked when upper management realizes that something is awry. Brutes are the most dangerous type of bullies. They are actually pre-felons, as they share criminal characteristics associated with pathological disorders.

- A male Brute can use hyperphysicality to threaten by leaning into the face of his target, taunting him with sudden movements, and pounding his fist on the table or desk.

Michelle's story about Jake, who had a pervasive disregard for others, shows an example of a Brute.

Michelle's Story

Jake, the president of a division at a major consumer products company, was known to become highly emotional and quasi-irrational if his ideas were questioned or his will was opposed. His drive, overconfidence, and strong opinions seemed to propel the division forward. The analysts were ecstatic over its performance, but within the division, misery reigned. Jake's key objective with the employees was to make sure they knew he had power over them, and he would invariably find a way to put the person he was talking to in his place.

One day, Michelle, a member of his leadership team, felt compelled to share information that was contrary to what she knew Jake thought to be true. She took a deep breath, and in a strong voice she began to articulate her concerns about a business decision that had been made. Jake glared at Michelle as others began to ask questions. His face got redder and redder until finally he slammed his fist on the table and began to scream and curse at Michelle for questioning his judgment. Surprised but not yet fearful, she once again listed her concerns and cited the research data that backed them up. With that, Jake jumped on the table and began yelling at her, hopping up and down to accentuate his point. Everyone else in the meeting froze until he stepped off the table and the meeting was over.

CRITICAL INCIDENT REPORT FOR MICHELLE'S STORY

Situation 1: Jake, president of a division of a consumer products company, has an overbearing, aggressive style of behavior. He abuses his position power over others by violating the standards of civility. His behavior goes unchecked because he has run his business successfully, and his revenues are at an all-time high. I am a very experienced product manager, and I have always considered part of my job to be on the outlook for problems and challenges and to bring them to the attention of my boss.

Behavior 1: I am a member of Jake's leadership team. In an effort to be accurate, I felt compelled during a meeting to offer a description of a problem that differed from Jake's view of it. Jake exploded with a barrage of verbal, vocal, and visual derogatory comments and gestures directed toward me. His words were threatening; his voice was loud and grew louder as he continued. His facial expressions were angry and mean. I tried to offer more facts to support my position. At that, Jake stood on the conference table as he continued yelling, and he jumped up and down as he pointed a finger at me and insulted my intelligence.

Consequence 1: Everyone at the meeting froze. They stared at their shoes and seemed to hold their breath until Jake stopped ranting and stepped off the conference table. The news spread like wildfire. Some considered calling security but didn't. Others started updating their résumés. Still others thought to report the incident to HR but didn't.

Michelle was going to have a talk with her boss come what may. She followed him back to his office.

MICHELLE'S SCRIPT

Jake: [Still incensed when he realized she had followed him to his office.] What do you want?

Michelle: To save you from a lawsuit.

Jake: [Jake takes a breath.] What?

Michelle: Do you realize how inappropriate your behavior was at that meeting?

Jake: I did not hire you to judge my behavior.

Michelle: Do you realize that your behavior could have caused a 911 call by anyone on the team, who could have reported to the police that you were displaying not only signs of severe emotional distress but also signs of violence? [Michelle has caught the Brute's attention here by calmly referencing the law.]

Jake: [Silence.]

Michelle: You seemed really upset. Help me understand why. Is it because you believe that we don't appreciate the importance of the project? [Michelle is giving him time to settle down and catch himself so he can have a moment of introspection to deal with his emotional imbalance. Unfortunately, the Brute has built up his self-worth by yelling at people and putting them down, so Michelle must remain calm, go slow, and stay in the conversation. If Michelle does this successfully once or twice, she will make a breakthrough in communication. She must not get angry or yell back. She shouldn't be a doormat either. She must depersonalize it.]

Jake: Upset?

Michelle: Yes, upset. You were yelling, calling people names, being mean, and we do not know why.

Jake: Yes, I am upset. [By now the Brute should have settled down. If not, Michelle should leave the space if he remains hostile and document the incident.]

Michelle: I am happy to listen. [By directly confronting the Brute and asking why he is upset, Michelle has an opportunity to defuse his anger. Of course, Michelle could have been told to leave his office in the worst-case scenario. At least she tried to deal with it in the moment to defuse his anger.]

YOUR BRUTE SCRIPT

What is expected:

_____

_____

_____

What is observed:

_____

_____

_____

CRITICAL INCIDENT 1

Situation:

_____

_____

_____

Behavior:

_____

_____

_____

Consequence:

_____

_____

_____

You say:

_____

_____

_____

The Brute may say:

_____

_____

_____

Your response:

_____

_____

_____

Critical Incident 2

Situation:

_____

_____

_____

Behavior:

_____

_____

_____

Consequence:

_____

_____

_____

You say:

_____

_____

_____

The Brute may say:

_____

_____

_____

Your response:

_____

_____

_____

The Brute needs to understand that it is not just the content of her rants but the way she is communicating that is the problem. Remember to put aside any emotion you may be feeling—or are receiving—and address the Brute's emotions head-on in a respectful way. If the Brute's rant is in front of others, it may be difficult to deal with the situation in the moment other than to make sure it doesn't get worse by responding emotionally or angrily. If her anger escalates, excuse yourself from the exchange or stop the meeting. Then arrange a later time to discuss the incident; this gives you time to write out your critical incident documentation.

Dealing with Brutes requires continuous interventions. Their bullying ways are deeply ingrained in their personal style. Some Brutes, with their inflated sense of self-importance, actually believe they are effectively leading others when they are behaving like a bully.

Sadly, if the Brute is a senior executive, it can set the tone for behavior and deference that can infect the entire organization, thus suppressing the creativity and energy that fuel growth in both an organization and an individual.

CEOs must purge this type of bully from the organization sooner rather than later, if not immediately, no matter how witty, intelligent, or capable the bully may appear to be. Because it is optimal not to hire a Brute in the first place, we recommend the use of a reliable assessment instrument as part of the checklist for the selection of candidates to work in your organization. The DISC and Hogan assessment instruments help sort out important aspects of an applicant's profile, such as a tendency to refuse to conform to company norms, impulsiveness and embedded aggression, hidden anger and/or anxiety, and disdain for complying with established responsibilities and promises.

Barbara Anne's Story

Barbara Anne was a brilliant actuary and CPA in an accounting firm. Based on her record of accomplishment, she was moved up to a position in management during a time of change in the organizational structure. Barbara Anne was known for her attention to detail, a masterful understanding of her clients' businesses and how a project could enhance their success, and good relations with the people she interacted with. She was now a manager with five reports and a new boss; her old boss with whom she had a very productive and respectful relationship retired.

Tray, Barbara Anne's new boss, was very senior in the firm and known for his insistence that projects be completed on time and within budget. He was also known for his abrasive style, although he was never confronted about it in the office, and he often demonstrated poor interpersonal skills. At the firm, he was seen as someone who had reached his highest level, and he felt bitter about that.

Barbara Anne's style of work was very thorough and methodical. Tray perceived her as being too slow; he did not appreciate the accuracy that resulted from her comprehensive analysis set out with reasonable time lines. Anybody working for Tray knew that he had difficulty listening and, because of his antisocial tendencies, that he was often very abrupt and disrespectful to others. To meet his need to control the work and the behavior of others, he closed down any attempts to create collaborative interactions. In other words, his motto was "Do your work, and do whatever I want you to do." Barbara Anne was accustomed to a collaborative relationship with her boss and often had additional, and in her view important, information to contribute as a project was rolled out.

Tray also had a habit of calling his reports nicknames. Sometimes he would use people's last name in a harsh tone of voice. Sometimes he would just refer to them as "butt-heads" if male and "dodo birds" if female. Tray called Barbara Anne "Tick-Tock" to remind her to work faster.

Barbara Anne felt disrespected by the nickname. As time passed, she felt increasingly compelled to say something about it. In the hallway one day, as Tray passed her, he called her Tick-Tock. She stopped him and said, "Tray, my name is Barbara Anne Fowler, and I prefer to be called Barbara Anne." One witness to this said you could hear the silence—it was deafening. Like a coiled cobra, Tray attacked, "I will call you anything I want, Fowler. In fact, I will call you 'Fowl' today and anything else I want tomorrow." Barbara Anne felt the world shrink around her. This was round 1, and the Brute clearly had her in his sights now.

Everyone who worked for Tray knew that not only was he interpersonally inept and overly demanding, he was also emotionally unpredictable, using words that were aggressive, nasty, and quasi-physically threatening. He was not remorseful about his name-calling or about his aggressive response to Barbara Anne. The irony was that he was seen as pleasant, civil, and even cordial when speaking to executives of higher rank, but he felt no shame in verbally abusing, humiliating, embarrassing, and diminishing his people's sense of personal worth.

Over the next weeks, on a daily basis, Tray kept calling Barbara Ann by her nickname. She became less sharp on the job. Not only were details slipping from her grasp, managing her people became increasingly difficult. When her team saw Tray's brutish behavior toward her increase, she lost the team's respect. Some team members started doing an end run around Barbara Anne and going to Tray directly for guidance in their work. Other members of her team started "yessing" her for anything she asked and then doing whatever they liked. They were cordial when they had to interact with her, but they avoided her as much as they could. The team's dismissal of her authority eroded Barbara Anne's confidence even more.

As the months passed, Barbara Anne heard a nagging voice inside her that continued to say, "You have to do something about this." But she did not know what to do. Getting completely involved in her work seemed like it would bring her some comfort, but instead it only made things worse. Now she was seen as a micromanager, and her team resented her for "nosing in" on their work. When a team member complained to Tray about this, he told Barbara Anne she was badgering her team members. She was at her wits' end. She hated getting up in the morning to go to work, something she had never experienced. She felt ill in her stomach most of the time, and she lacked energy. This lethargy caused her to take more sick days than she would normally take. Her doctor recommended medication to ease the symptoms, but its side effects further complicated matters with sleeplessness, which caused more fatigue at work. When she returned from a sick day, Tray made it a point to swing by her office and tell her that things really went smoothly while she was away, implying she was not needed or missed at work. Her team members picked up on this and began ignoring her even more. She overheard them saying that she was not doing her job.

Barbara Anne was physically spent, emotionally drained, and psychologically depressed. The workplace had become the loneliest place in the world. Tray continued his brutish bullying at meetings, using verbal reprimands without real cause. He would make negative comments about her competence and lack of knowledge. He was always disagreeable with her no matter what the topic of conversation. His negative and irritable tension around her was escalating as well. He would bristle visibly whenever she spoke. Barbara Anne's confidence was decimated. She felt totally rejected and increasingly more vulnerable to the bullying. Worse, she began to feel incompetent. She considered her options. She doubted Tray would dismiss her, so she considered quitting or asking for a different role.

But Barbara Anne had enough energy for one more round. She went to Tray's boss to seek advice. Not only did Tray's boss turn a blind eye to the situation, he left it completely to Tray to sort it out. At that point, Barbara Anne invested in an executive career coach to help her out of the situation. She landed a job at another firm after six long months.

Perhaps there was another possible outcome for Barbara Anne. Here's how she could have dealt with Tray. Her four critical incident reports (based on the CIT[1]) and script follow.

CRITICAL INCIDENT REPORT 1 FOR BARBARA ANNE'S STORY

Situation 1: Tray, our boss, has the habit of nicknaming everyone and using those nicknames during team meetings. I never liked having a nickname because I thought it unprofessional and demeaning. As I walked down the hallway, and he was coming from the other direction, he addressed me using his nickname for me. I felt the need to correct him right then, so I stopped to share my preference that he use my actual name, not a nickname. The behavioral exchange is next.

Behavior 1: I said, "Tray, my name is Barbara Anne Fowler, and I prefer to be called Barbara Anne." Tray attacked in a loud voice with, "I will call you anything I want, Fowler. In fact, I will call you 'Fowl' today and anything else I want tomorrow."

Consequence 1: I felt verbally abused, humiliated, embarrassed, and diminished in front of several people in cubicles. From that moment on, I have not received a kind word or any positive reinforcement from Tray for my work. On the contrary, for the rest of that day and the next two days after that, Tray found any excuse he could to come by my work area to use the nickname, repeating it over and over again, with a louder voice each time.

CRITICAL INCIDENT REPORT 2 FOR BARBARA ANNE'S STORY

Situation 2: As the weeks went on, I was greatly affected by Tray's behavior. I wanted to do something about it, but the truth was I did not know what to do. I threw myself into my work, but I am now seen as a micromanager by my team, who resent me for getting involved in their work. When one team member complained to Tray about this, he used this in his negative narrative against me.

Behavior 2: Without seeing the irony of his statement, Tray pounced on me again, saying I was badgering my team members. He stated, "Maybe you did not have enough of your own work to do," which to me implied that I could not prioritize. When I tried to set up a one-on-one meeting with him to clear the air and to find out exactly what about my work he was criticizing, he refused to meet. He said, "Bring it up at the team meeting."

Consequence 2: I felt like there was nothing I could do right. I felt ill in my stomach most of the time and experienced a severe lack of energy. My doctor recommended medication to ease the symptoms, but the side effects further complicated matters with sleeplessness, which caused more fatigue at work.

CRITICAL INCIDENT REPORT 3
FOR BARBARA ANNE'S STORY

Situation 3: When I returned from a sick day, Tray made it a point to swing by my office.

Behavior 3: While standing in my doorway, Tray said, "Things really went smoothly while you were away." He sarcastically added, "You don't have to worry about the work not getting done when you are away." Then he walked off.

Consequence 3: I felt put down, badgered, and demeaned at work. I felt I was being isolated. Some of my team members, having heard these comments from Tray, soon developed a mindset that not only was I not needed at work but also that I was not doing my job. I became physically spent, emotionally drained, psychologically depressed, and felt all alone.

CRITICAL INCIDENT REPORT 4
FOR BARBARA ANNE'S STORY

Situation 4: I suffered repeated bullying at meetings and in the work area.

Behavior 4: Tray continued his bullying at meetings, using verbal reprimands without real cause. He would make negative comments about my supposed incompetence and lack of knowledge. They were the same comments over and over again; his repetition reinforced his negative opinion of me in everyone's awareness every day. That deepened my team's misperception of my abilities and me. He was always disagreeable with me at meetings, no matter what the topic of conversation was. It seemed that his negative and irritable tension around me was escalating as well. He would bristle visibly whenever I spoke.

Consequence 4: I went to Tray's boss to share my situation and seek help. I told him that I felt afraid of Tray's escalating behavior. His boss told me in no uncertain terms that it was up to Tray to sort this out. Now, I felt completely abandoned.

BARBARA ANNE'S SCRIPT

Barbara Anne: Tray, I set up this meeting with you to discuss optimizing my productivity at work.

Tray: [Interrupts.] Good.

Barbara Anne: Yes, it is important we talk about this. I have been with the company for over 10 years. During that time, working in other parts of the company, I have come to expect that communication here is conducted in a manner that enhances productivity. I've always loved working here, and I have a deep sense of loyalty to the company and its mission largely because of the respect that we all hold for each other. When the reorganization occurred, I was excited about the opportunity to work for you, and I expected to learn from you. What I have observed in our interpersonal exchanges, as well as in your interpersonal exchanges with others on the team, is an insistence on using demeaning nicknames with all of us. [She should pause to see if he tries to defend using nicknames. If he does, she should listen politely but say that she does not consider it respectful and she has not seen it done in other parts of the company.]

Tray: [Glares at her in silence.]

Barbara Anne: I am very open to feedback. If my attempts to be very detailed and careful with my work rub up against your need to have quick results and fast turnarounds, I am willing to work with you to achieve quicker results while maintaining quality. In fact, in a respectful conversation I am sure we can reach a happy compromise on understanding how better to work together. We have style differences, and I can understand that may have caused you to become impatient and frustrated. [Barbara Ann should stop talking and wait for a response.]

Tray: [Silence.]

Barbara Anne: For me, using a nickname to make your point is a demeaning and derogatory way of communicating. I would like to suggest better ways of communication so that I might get my work done in a productive, efficient, and effective way to better meet your expectations. I'd like to establish a more positive relationship with you so that together we can meet the needs of the organization. Will you agree on a more collaborative exchange between us?

Tray: [Reluctantly.] You have to be far more responsive to meet my needs and the needs of the company.

Barbara Anne: [She does not get derailed here.] Will you agree to stop using nicknames in our interactions?

Tray: Most people enjoy their nicknames. You are way too sensitive.

Barbara Anne: Please agree with me to create a more collaborative relationship and stop using nicknames in our exchanges. Maybe we can meet more regularly to discuss your timetables on different projects I am working on. I will set these meetings up with your assistant. [If Tray does not behave in a more collaborative way and continues to use nicknames, Barbara Anne should document another critical incident for future use should she need it. The Brute is rarely calmed down in one meeting.]

SCRIPT FOR DEALING WITH ANGER

Here's a script for dealing with a Brute's anger:

Brute: [In a harsh tone of voice.] Why are you interrupting me? What is wrong with you?

Target: [In a poised and polite voice.] You seem upset. [Present tense.] Help me understand why.

Brute: I am not upset.

Target: You seemed upset. [Past tense.] Why?

Brute: Maybe I am stressed and too busy for the kind of interruptions I am forced to endure.

Target: Did something go differently from what you expected?

Brute: The financials from accounting were not sent to the board on time.

Target: What needs to be done to remedy the situation?

Brute: [Explains the logistics, the personnel involved, and what needs to be done while calming down.]

Target: If you would like me to have someone help you, I can find a person. Then tomorrow, I would like to explain in detail why I showed up today because I need your help. Agreed? [You have defused the moment, but you've also let the Brute know there is still more to discuss about his behavior.]

Brute: Yes. Thanks. [There is a possibility that the Brute could behave in a very aggressive manner. He may appear violent. If so, immediately get up and leave the room. If necessary, call security.]

SPECIFIC TIPS TO USE WHEN CONFRONTING A BRUTE

- Remember, a Brute is probably operating from an oversized ego and an empathy-deficit disorder. One must not take his behavior personally.

- If possible, address in the moment the bully's negative emotion or anger to try to understand why she is so upset. One example might be to say, "You seem upset. [Pause and wait for a moment.] Help me understand." A chance to reflect on her emotional state may help her to self-correct.

- In working with a difficult leader, should you uncover information that might be either controversial or contrary to his point of view, consider having a pre-meeting with him to discuss the data. This may also be done in a post-meeting where the leader's ego is not publicly threatened.

- Do not be a bystander. Most Brutes are indiscriminate about whom to target and will often switch to someone else, depending on the issue and their mood. So you could be next! Discuss the incident you witnessed with the Brute and offer ideas, solutions, and support. If the bullying escalates, bring the situation to the attention of a leader or human resources. Have courage, and you will benefit from feeling proud that you haven't been a silent and unwilling accomplice to inappropriate workplace behavior.

- If after confronting the Brute, her bullying continues, determine who is the best person or body of people to speak to about the Brute and do so with documented and dated critical incidents.

CHECKLIST OF THE BRUTE'S BEHAVIORAL CHARACTERISTICS

☐ Criticizes aggressively, causing a hostile workplace and deflated morale

☐ Disrupts progress by overtalking to demonstrate power

☐ Violates boundaries with improper comments and invading personal space

☐ Expresses intimidation with words, tone of voice, and facial expressions

☐ Uses threats to put others down

☐ Is overly demanding

- [ ] Is insincere

- [ ] Is disingenuous

- [ ] Is interpersonally inept

- [ ] Violates targets' personal rights

- [ ] Is irritable and aggressive in interactions

- [ ] Barrages targets with rapid-fire accusations

- [ ] Refuses to use positive team behaviors, such as seeking and listening to others' opinions

- [ ] Disrupts and deprives others of joy on the job

- [ ] Breaks promises and is dishonest

- [ ] Breaks rules of engagement by making up his own

- [ ] Disregards work-life balance

- [ ] Embarrasses and diminishes others' sense of personal worth

- [ ] Reprimands others without reason

- [ ] Impulsively humiliates targets in front of others

- [ ] Introduces fear into relationships to the point of terrorizing others

- [ ] Abuses position power over employees

- [ ] Displays observable immature hysteria

- [ ] Has an empathy-deficit disorder

- [ ] Hurts others to avoid being hurt

☐ Has no remorse or guilt after he has hurt someone

☐ Is emotionally unpredictable

☐ Acts with excessive anger and hostility

☐ Always blames others when things go wrong

If you have checked eight or more of the items on this list, you are undoubtedly dealing with a Brute.

WHEN ALL ELSE
FAILS . . . GET HELP

The bully survives on your silence.
—Christine Farrell Crotty[1]

You have confronted the bully, but it did not work. Now what? The short answer is that you have an even greater opportunity to develop your character, as continuing to deal with the problem will test your tenacity and determination to practice civility in your situation. In this chapter we will discuss who can be helpful to you if your own attempts to remediate the bullying are unsuccessful. We will share what the law says about workplace bullying, referred to as "abusive supervision, incivility, and creating a hostile work environment." Dealing with bullying is a complicated task. It is OK to get help.

The antidote for fifty enemies is one friend.
—ARISTOTLE

The first and most logical person to discuss being bullied with is your boss. But if your boss is the bully, this is not the most practical first step. You also need to consider whether your boss or boss' boss favors the individual who is bullying you. If so, she may not be able to be objective—and you'll want to consider other options for getting help.

If you think your boss or boss' boss can be impartial, you need to figure out whether she is aware of the bullying behavior and the impact it is having on you. Set up a time to meet with her when you know you will have her full attention. There are several important parts to the conversation:

- Assure her of your loyalty to her and the company. You might express how much you value your work, what you have learned and hope to learn from her and your colleagues, and your general satisfaction with the job. This will put her at ease, knowing that you aren't a flight risk, and make it easier for her to listen and support the conversation.

- State that recently, as she may be aware, you have found yourself the subject of some ridicule, taunting, yelling, and so on, and you are finding it difficult to get your work done and stay positive. Tell her that you have analyzed the situation. You have documented the incidents, met with the bully, and expressed your feelings about the impact of his behavior, but it has not worked, and the bully's behavior has not changed.

- You would like advice on how best to handle the situation and are asking for information that you may not already have to give you more context. If you have done something that provoked the bullying, you would like to remedy it. If the bully is under pressure that you are unaware of and is taking it out on you, you would like advice on tactics to better handle it in the moment.

- Listen to your boss's feedback and advice. Determine whether the bullying is being caused by events out of your control or if there is something you can do to address the situation. If so, ask for ideas that might be helpful either to tolerate the behavior or to confront it.

- Conclude the meeting with the assurance that you enjoy your job and wish to remain as productive as possible. Ask if it is OK to check in from time to time to get feedback and further assistance if necessary.

Several things have been accomplished in this meeting. First, you have demonstrated that you are a committed and hardworking person who wishes only to continue supporting your boss and the company. Second, you are putting this person on notice that something is occurring that is eroding your ability to perform. Third, you are soliciting help and advice along with feedback on how you can address the situation more effectively.

If your boss or boss's boss is unresponsive, unwilling, or unable to help you, the person you approach after your boss must be trustworthy, someone who will receive the information without retaliating. Again, your concerns must be presented in light of their impact on your productivity, that of the team, and the company— not your personal gain. In other words, you must convey that if this kind of bullying behavior is allowed to continue, it will slow down the productivity of both you *and* others in the organization. It must be made clear that your personal agenda is to be able to contribute to the best of your ability to the goals and mission of the organization.

STAKEHOLDERS

Here is a list of stakeholders you might consider taking into your confidence as you pursue dealing with the bully.

Witnesses

Anyone who happens to be around during the bullying, has seen you being bullied, or is also a target of your bully can be an excellent ally with whom to collaborate on steps for prevention. Note the times that the witness has seen the bullying behavior. Ask him if he agrees with you that these are, in fact, bullying incidents.

If there is agreement, determine a way the witness can intercede on your behalf and vice versa. Interrupting and redirecting the conversation is one way a witness can reduce the volume of the bullying. If the witness is unsure about whether the incidents constitute bullying, ask for clarification, feedback, and advice in case you are mistaken about the severity of the bullying and its impact and are perhaps taking it too personally.

Trusted Colleagues

Because they know you and the organization in which you work, these coworkers may be able to suggest ways to better respond to the situation or help put the bullying you are experiencing into perspective. If you take them into your confidence and ask for their advice, they may also be supportive in the moment.

Keep the number of colleagues you share your concerns with to just a few people. These individuals should be well respected and known for their integrity and discretion in the organization. The more politically savvy they are, the more able they will be to make helpful suggestions for next steps that won't stir up too many emotions or cause future difficulty for you with the bully.

Leadership Team Members

These people are typically closer to the ground and will see and hear bullying behavior before human resources becomes aware of it. They can be approached if others have been spoken to and have not taken any action. The most obvious member to approach is the person in the direct chain of command to the bully.

Documentation is critical for these individuals. Your tone of voice has to be controlled and objective. Your conversation should begin with a statement of loyalty to the company. They probably will want to address it immediately, so make sure you have positioned your complaint in terms of productivity lost and the impact on you and others.

Human Resources

Human resources promises to secure and promote a healthy working environment for employees. But if you don't have specific examples of both the harassment and the steps you have already taken to remediate the situation, they may see your complaint as frivolous and you as lacking in emotional maturity.

Human resources needs to see that you have made an attempt to confront the bully yourself. The critical incidents you documented and the scripts you developed will be very helpful here. The critical incidents are the best way to motivate HR to treat your case as important. If human resources itself has not succumbed to a culture of bullying, they should intervene immediately and speak to the bully and her boss. One intervention they can employ is hiring an executive coach to work with the bully. In the intake part of the process, the 360 stakeholder interviews will reveal to the bully when she receives the feedback that she is perceived as a bully and not a leader. This feedback will certainly catch her attention and may prompt her to remediate her behavior.

The CEO and/or Board of Directors

The CEO or board should be approached only as a last resort. There are measured and appropriate ways to do this. It is a drastic step, and it must be handled very carefully and with enormous political savvy.

As the governing body of a company, a board's primary job is to select, support, appoint, and review the performance of the CEO. Their overarching responsibility is a fiduciary one, ensuring that the company is well run for the benefit of its shareholders. However, in their oversight of the CEO and their responsibility to measure and review his performance on a regular basis, it would be natural for them to be informed of any behaviors that were harming the integrity or reputation of the organization. More and more boards are being held responsible for anything that could potentially negatively influence the company via a failure of the CEO to take action, such as an ongoing bullying case. Bullying in the workplace is also getting more and more attention from law firms. Some see it as a new field for business development.

It is our recommendation that the situation be presented in a letter to the board of directors. It is likely that the board will be very concerned. In addition to presenting the facts objectively, it is imperative that you do not use litigious language. The bullying itself will capture their attention. If you have gotten to this level, it is possible that you will also suffer a penalty. Whistle-blowers are often brave and courageous spokespeople who are acting on behalf of the company. Yet they find that whether they are listened to or not, they no longer fit in or are accepted after their revelations are made public. Be prepared to risk your job if you take this step.

An Attorney

If you feel you must leave the company because the bullying has made your life miserable, consult with an attorney to determine the steps you need to take to get a severance package. Make sure the lawyer is not known to be immediately litigious so that you can work out an amicable separation with the company. She will advise you on how and whom to approach to negotiate your separation. If no action is taken, she can intercede on your behalf.

Bullying is the opposite of fair play. Bullying can cause the target to feel that he has been treated unfairly. This lowers serotonin levels (low levels of serotonin have been linked to poor decision-making[2]), resulting in that kicked-in-the-gut feeling, which can compromise performance. Fair play is essential. It frames business arrangements with integrity. Integrity speaks to honesty and ethical decision-making that occurs when one acts in good faith with others in all dealings for a company.

Professionals with integrity refrain from making false, misleading, and deceptive statements, and they provide accurate information. They avoid conflict-of-interest relationships such as giving expensive gifts, bribery, and supporting a person who is favored for a position that another who is less liked but more qualified won't get.

Adhering to this high standard of leadership behavior means sharing credit for work accomplishments and being worthy of trust. A professional can't ever give too much credit to those who do the work, and she must build trust by honoring all contracts, promises, and commitments. We must respect the intrinsic worth of people at work and provide an environment where there is an expectation that this respect will manifest in all conversations, especially in those which have to do with addressing conflict, solving problems, and making decisions. Keeping your word is not just the right thing to do. It is a critical ingredient for the stability of transactions between and among professionals. Your word is your bond.

WOMEN BULLYING WOMEN

Brenda's Story

Brenda was curled up in a fetal position one night after work. The agony she was experiencing in the office finally shot through her body. It was concentrated in her stomach, and she could not move. Her tears had come and gone, and she lay spent on her bed, in the dark, thinking for the hundredth time what she possibly could have done to deserve the constant and repeated mistreatment she was receiving from her boss.

A communications major in college, Brenda got her dream job 10 years into her career. She'd worked in retail, marketing, and public relations when a major bank called and asked her to join its marketing department. Her salary almost doubled, and her excitement about learning from the pros at the bank, especially her boss, a woman with 25 years of notable experience, was palpable. She came to work eager and willing to begin her training anew in a far more sophisticated environment than those she had worked in previously.

The marketing group had just moved to a new space on the second floor of the old bank building that housed the corporate headquarters. Brenda felt a sense of awe. She walked through the ornate steel front gates and down the vestibule of the building with its 20-foot ceilings, painted in a rococo style. Marble statues of the ancient Romans lined the front, and a grand marble staircase led from the hall to the second floor of the bank. Down the hall, the marketing group was assembled in small offices, each with a window, surrounding a large area where the administrative assistants worked in an open space.

Brenda couldn't wait to see her office, and she was shocked when her female boss led her down a side hall to a small windowless closet with a desk and chair and told her to get herself situated. A team meeting began 30 minutes later, and after Brenda was introduced, she again was dismayed to find that she was not assigned any work. When Brenda raised her hand to ask for her assignment, her boss informed her that after a bank orientation that morning, she would be told what project she was going to work on.

Brenda completed her orientation and returned to her office in the late afternoon, popped her head into the boss's office to say she was back, and then waited in her small, dark office for the next step. It never came. The next morning,

Brenda came to the office convinced that the first day was an anomaly, and she asked her boss again what she would be working on. Her boss gave her some reading materials and examples of some of the team's past campaigns and told her to go back to her office. Brenda was acutely aware of how isolating her physical situation was seen by others. She walked to the coffee area in the large space several times, hoping to engage one of her colleagues. They all seemed very busy and paid no attention to her. This treatment continued into the second week. Brenda was given a filing assignment. She ran a few errands, but she spent most of her time alone.

She became determined to figure out a plan on how to become a true member of the team. At the weekly meetings, she spoke up with ideas or possible solutions that occurred to her only to be silenced by her boss, who said, "When you have been here longer, you will earn the right to speak."

A month went by. Brenda still had no work. She knew one of the vice presidents in another department and asked for a meeting so she could discuss her situation. He was sympathetic but reminded her that her boss had been with the bank for 25 years and was highly regarded by the CEO. In fact, he said, she could do no wrong as far as the CEO was concerned.

Not wanting to make matters worse and fearful of a negative reaction, Brenda decided not to complain to human resources but to stick it out. Her discouragement morphed into anger, and after the third month of being isolated by the entire team and specifically by her boss, she decided she would wait to be fired rather than give her the satisfaction of quitting. At the end of the third month, she was given her notice with two weeks' pay. She left, still stymied and deeply hurt by the whole event that made no sense.

What was going on?

Brenda's boss had personally hired her, but—almost like buyer's remorse—had come to doubt her decision and subsequently began resenting her. During the interview she said that she too had come out of retail marketing, and she implied that she respected that part of Brenda's background the most. Brenda was 15 years younger, very smart, and always professionally and stylishly dressed. Her boss was overweight and dressed frumpily. Brenda was raised in a wealthy suburb of New York City. Her boss was raised in a working-class area of the Bronx, a New York City borough. Brenda went to an Ivy League university. Her boss went to a city college. Brenda was happily married to a very successful trader. Her boss had never been married. Brenda was no match for this woman who took out all her jealous insecurities on Brenda from the moment she joined the team. The other members of the team were intimidated by Brenda as well, and they took their lead from the boss and silently ostracized her too.

Why did this go on for so long?

Her boss had set up Brenda to fail. The longer Brenda worked at the bank without producing results, the more she could justify her lack of value. The bullying started the first day and successfully achieved its goal of intimidation and oppression. As Brenda moved from surprise to dismay and then to anger, she only cemented her worthlessness in her boss's eyes and those of team. The boss, through her close relationship with the CEO, had created immunity for herself. No one was willing to stand up to her or to support Brenda and condemn her unfair treatment.

MISTAKES FROM WHICH TO LEARN

Brenda wasn't fully appreciative of the value that she had brought to the bank. Her self-doubt about the relevance of her prior experience combined with her awe and reverence for the bank and the opportunity it had provided her made her question herself and quickly eroded her self-esteem. She became the perfect target for the boss, who was bullying Brenda because of who she was, not her inability to do the job. She had had different experiences, but they were still valuable. If she had documented her major accomplishments and the skills that she used to achieve them, she would have reminded herself of her value and blamed herself less for the job's not working out.

Brenda should have protested the placement of her office the first week. By insisting that she should have been placed closer to the team, she could have switched with a researcher or admin who would have benefited from the quiet isolation of her office. She could have taken this early on to human resources as a more benign issue of space planning and alerted them in a preliminary but more discreet way to her situation.

Brenda could have used her downtime to get out of her office and meet with key stakeholders in the bank. After introducing herself and her background, she could have asked them what they needed from marketing, when their experiences with the department had gone well and when they could have gone better. Brenda could have written a short white paper on the results of her interviews and shared it with her boss as an attempt to prove her value and commitment. In this meeting, she could have demonstrated her collaborative skills and desire to make a positive difference.

A long-term employee might have benefited financially from waiting it out until she was fired, but that is not what we would recommend. Brenda had her whole career in front of her, and the two weeks of salary she received when she was fired hardly mattered to her. She dug her heels in and suffered three months of intolerable treatment from a woman who was unable to control her emotions. She could have taken her dignity and her résumé out the door after the situation was clear and saved herself a great deal of angst and the erosion of her self-esteem. When a bully is protected by the powers that be, there is no recourse but to leave and find new employment. Brenda's last act could have been to conduct an exit interview with human resources so that a record of her boss's bullying behavior could be established.

MOBBING

Henry's Story

Henry had had irritable bowel syndrome since childhood. He had learned how to control the painful episodes he experienced on a regular basis with diet, exercise, and meditation. As a result, he was thinner than he wanted to be, but he was strong and healthy. Because of his illness, he decided to become a nurse, and he took extra courses to gain admission to a top nursing school. He received a second bachelor's degree in nursing. He was a straight-A student and was immediately hired by a major hospital as a day nurse on the oncology floor. He relished his work, and he enthusiastically arrived each morning excited about what he was doing, working alongside other nurses and doctors for whom he had enormous respect.

It was a regular part of the nurses' routine to order in lunch each day. All the nurses quickly ascertained that Henry did not eat the same foods they ate as a group. The nurses tended to be stress eaters, and they ordered relatively fattening foods for lunch, accompanied by French fries, chips, and often a dessert. Henry ordered a salad each day.

Henry confided to one of the nurses with whom he had become friendly that he had irritable bowel syndrome and that he was lactose intolerant and had to be extra careful about what he ate. It was, therefore, shocking to Henry that shortly after sharing this confidence, the nurses as a group started putting pressure on him to eat unhealthy foods that were strictly forbidden by his diet. They would hand him a plate of French fries or order him a milkshake. They made the daily lunch together a deeply unpleasant experience for Henry. Their taunting went from pushing food on him to teasing him about his diet and weight. After weeks of this teasing, Henry finally asked for a transfer to another unit and never again shared his condition with anyone at work.

What was going on?

Group bullying, called *mobbing*, is like a contagion and feeds upon itself. Henry triggered unprofessional and ultimately brutish bullying from his peers for no apparent reason. The insecurity of the group about weight and physical fitness was underscored by the presence of an individual who, for health reasons, had curtailed his eating choices and exercised regularly to stay fit. All this from a group of nurses who were in the healthcare profession!

Mobbing is a real phenomenon that you can fall into if you are not mindful of what you tolerate at work. If you don't stand up against this kind of behavior, especially in high-stress environments—such as the oncology unit in a busy hospital—people will forget to be civil and kind to one another.

What could Henry have done?

As in the case of the Belier, Henry needed to identify the ringleader of the abuse and take her aside. By confronting her with documented critical incidents about the pain and anguish the mobbing was causing him, perhaps he could have appealed to her sensitivities. Henry could have approached each member of the team separately and asked for understanding after explaining his situation.

Last, this situation could have been resolved by human resources. A timely team intervention might have defused the stresses and pressures being experienced by the nurses who were triggering their hostile reactions to Henry.

LEGAL SUPPORT FOR DEALING WITH A BULLY

Bullying is not a cause for legal action in American civil courts *currently*, but we anticipate that it is just a matter of time. Eleven states have antibullying laws pending. Also, there are antibullying laws in Australia, England, France, Germany, Sweden, Switzerland, and the Canadian province of Quebec. Margaret R. Kohut, a certified criminal justice specialist, reported that two court actions have been taken in the United States.[3]

In 1998, two Supreme Court decisions made employers responsible for harassment and discrimination by employees who were acting as agents of the employer, such as middle managers and supervisors. *Burlington Industries v. Ellerth* and *Faragher v. City of Boca Raton* both established liability for senior management for the abusive behavior of their employees. Kohut goes on to report that in 2005, a bullying Indianapolis surgeon was held responsible to the tune of $325,000. In 2006, in a defamation law-suit filed against a school district, a teacher received a settlement of $500,000.

Currently, anyone who is bullied at work, has little to no legal recourse unless the target has been discriminated against because of his or her protected status of nationality, race, religion, age, or specifics covered by the Americans with Disabilities Act of 1990, the Age Discrimination in Employment Act of 1967, or the Civil Rights Act of 1964. Although harassment that causes a hostile work environment may very well violate these three laws, there needs to be an antibullying law that does not require protected status. It should cover all types of bullying behavior in the work environment without regard to the acts referenced. As of 2015, California requires companies with over 50 employees to provide training to managers on how to prevent bullying behavior at work, but bullying still isn't illegal. Utah also passed legislation in 2015 mandating training for state agency employees only.

Whereas petty slights and annoyances do not rise to the level of illegality, the four types of bullying behavior we describe in this book are most likely to be considered unlawful. All four create a work environment that would be intimidating, hostile, and offensive to a reasonable person.

Those offensive behaviors can be any of the following. (1) For example, the false rumor mongering, gossiping, and lying of the *Belier* is defamation, and it includes both libel and slander. *Libel* is the written form of defamation, which is very much on the increase in this social media age, and *slander* consists of spoken statements that mislead or deceive. (2) The interference of productive work performance by the *Blocker* is another category of offensive behavior through which the bully prevents talent in the company from performing at their best by controlling all the functions at work and never allowing the targets to grow on the job. (3) The *Braggart's* overly expressive, self-absorbed grandstanding and derogatory joking at others' expense burns up the positive energy by diverting attention that could be focused on work and instead holds it captive by an unhealthy ego. The company pays a high cost because the Braggart prevents people from being productive. (4) The *Brute's* offensive, antisocial, overaggressive behavior, seen in his or her name-calling, slurs, epithets, insults, put-downs, aggressive threats, and intimidating tactics, creates a hostile work environment for the target and others.

Some believe that accountability through the law is the only way to eliminate workplace bullying. But there is much that managers can do within their sphere of influence to ensure a bully-proof workplace.

I AM THE MANAGER, AND
I HAVE A BULLY ON MY TEAM:
WHAT DO I DO?

If you want to manage somebody, manage yourself.
Do that well and you'll be ready . . . to start leading.
—ANONYMOUS

It is essential for managers to model and communicate the appropriate rules of proper engagement to all the people who work on the team. Developing the skills of active listening, mindful empathy, and giving full attention to each other in conversation ensures a civil culture. If someone is exhibiting bullying behavior, you must address his actions directly. The proper mindset preparation, documenting critical incidents, and writing scripts are valuable and applicable when dealing with a bully on a team and can become part of the performance review process. Preparing a script to reprimand someone after a specific bullying event or if the behavior becomes too egregious is vital. A manager should be recording her own critical incidents when dealing with the bully. You may need to bring in others to assist, including human resources.

Before we prepare to engage the bully, let's look at the managers' responsibility in the execution of their duties as leaders, which is essential for a bully-proof workplace. Managers manage, but the managers have to lead as well, requiring different skills with either effort. The chart in Figure 8.1 features the four areas of a manager's responsibility. A good manager enables workers to use their full knowledge, skills, and capabilities.

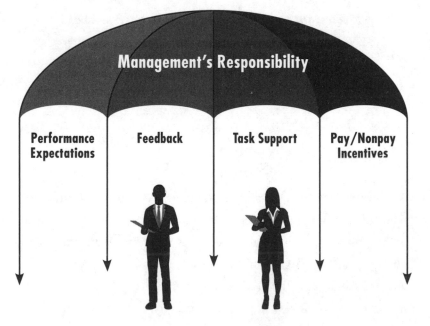

FIGURE 8.1 The Four Areas of a
Manager's Responsibility in a Bully-Proof Workplace

Potential bullies can start down the road toward bullying if they are operating from the *lack* of any one of the four categories of support that managers must provide to help their people meet the optimal level of job productivity. The categories are clear expectations, direct feedback, fair and appropriate support for tasks assigned, and pay and nonpay incentives. A potential bully might take the absence of these pillars of support personally as a slight; begin to misperceive the situation as unfair, which triggers his insecurities; and then start to retaliate against a subordinate or peer.

MANAGEMENT QUESTIONNAIRE

The following questionnaire has been adapted from one that appeared in Thomas Gilbert's book *Human Competence: Engineering Worthy Performance*.[1] A manager should answer the following questions to create a fair, productive, and bully-proof workplace. They are designed to identify areas of the work, work procedures, or work environment that are required for proper management.

Please respond yes or no to each item as it relates to your reports. For each no response, please recognize that your answer demonstrates a *lack* of connectivity with employees and should be addressed. If you give the survey to your employees and receive back more than five no responses, you must attend to it. It is management's responsibility to work toward creating the conditions to enable employees to answer yes to all these questions.

Management Skills

Using the following questions to optimize effectiveness and efficiency, management has to set expectations, build feedback systems, allocate task support, align processes and procedures, and decide on pay and nonpay incentives.[2]

EXPECTATIONS

- Are directions readily available to help experienced employees perform well?

- Are directions clear enough to help experienced employees perform well?

- Are directions accurate?

- Are directions free of confusion that slows performance and invites error?

- Are directions free of "data glut," and are the directions stripped down to their simplest form?

- Are directions consistent with good training practices?

- Are directions given in a timely manner?

- Do employees have all the information they need to do their job well?

- Are clear and measurable performance standards communicated so that employees know how well they are supposed to perform?

- Do employees believe the standards are reasonable?

FEEDBACK

- Does work-related feedback provided by employees describe results consistent or inconsistent with expectations?

- Does work-related feedback provided by supervisors describe results consistent or inconsistent with expectations?

- Is feedback immediate and frequent enough to help employees remember what they did?

- Is feedback selective and specific—limited to a few matters of importance and free of data glut and vague generalities?

- Is feedback educational—positive and constructively informative so that employees can learn from it?

TOOLS, EQUIPMENT, PROCEDURES, AND TASK SUPPORT

These tools include such supports as accurate scheduling, planning, allocations, resources, reference materials, and anything available to do a job well.

- Are there necessary tools, equipment, procedures, and task support available for the job?

- Are they reliable and efficient?

- Are they safe?

- Are procedures efficient, and do they avoid unnecessary steps?

- Are they based on sound methods rather than on tradition?

- Are they appropriate to the job and skill levels?

- Are they free of boring repetition?

- Are materials appropriate to the job?

- Is time sufficient to do the job well?

- Are the training and work areas conducive to being productive?

- Do employees complain about tools, equipment, and facilities? If so, what do they complain about?

PAY AND NONPAY INCENTIVES

- Is the pay for the job competitive?

- Are bonuses or raises given? Are they based on good performance?

- Does good performance bear a clear relationship to career advancement?

- Are meaningful nonpay incentives given, based on good results—not completion of assignments?

- Are nonpay incentives so infrequent as to be meaningless?

- Is good performance free of punishing consequences, such as peer pressure on employees who are successful or being asked to "pick up the slack" for someone else when they have finished a project early?

- Is the work environment free of incentives to perform poorly, such as praise for designing, developing, and delivering a project in record time without regard to content required for the project?

- Does a balance of positive versus negative incentives encourage good performance?

Leadership Skills

As John P. Kotter emphasized in *Accelerate*, management is critical, but it is not leadership.[3] Leadership is associated with taking the organization into the future by setting the vision for work through exemplary communication skills and the ability to adapt and not let ego get in the way, collaborating with others, integrating proper standards into decision-making, eliciting commitment from others by modeling proper interpersonal engagement skills, and having productive and positive relations with those who do the work. The following checklist unpacks the skills leaders need to master.

Do managers receive training in dialogue skills when promoted into management?

Yes ___ *No* ___

Can they actively listen conscientiously with openness and agreeableness?

Yes ___ *No* ___

Can they empathize with others and not let their ego overshadow the conversation?

Yes ___ *No* ___

Can they attend to others and be receptive to how they think, feel, and behave?

Yes ___ *No* ___

Can they diagnose, detail, discern, and make decisions with relative ease?

Yes ___ *No* ___

Can they engage others without losing emotional composure?

Yes ____ *No* ____

Can they remain respectful and resilient in times of conflict and when others vie for power?

Yes ____ *No* ____

Do managers receive training in interpersonal interactive skills when promoted into management?

Yes ____ *No* ____

Can they speak to groups or to an individual with specificity and clarity?

Yes ____ *No* ____

Can they communicate a problem directly so as not to project judgment or negativity?

Yes ____ *No* ____

Can they communicate a problem specifically, stating what is expected and what is observed?

Yes ____ *No* ____

Can they communicate a problem in a nonpunishing and non-threatening way?

Yes ____ *No* ____

Can they communicate a compelling message in which words, vocal tones, and facial expressions are aligned?

Yes ____ *No* ____

Do managers receive training in how to use their power when promoted into management?

Yes ____ *No* ____

Can they appropriately use position power without being coercive, inducing fear, or overusing sanctions?

Yes ___ *No* ___

Can they appropriately use political power without taking credit away from others or being insensitive?

Yes ___ *No* ___

Can they appropriately use interpersonal interactive skills without projecting negativity?

Yes ___ *No* ___

Can they appropriately use personal power skills: self-discipline, interest in people, and ability to provide feedback?

Yes ___ *No* ___

Can they appropriately use intrapersonal power skills: willingness to adapt, keep focused, and be engaged?

Yes ___ *No* ___

Do managers receive training in team skills when promoted into management?

Yes ___ *No* ___

Can they successfully complete tasks by:

Initiating new ideas?

Yes ___ *No* ___

Seeking information?

Yes ___ *No* ___

Seeking the opinion of others?

Yes ___ *No* ___

Sharing information?

Yes ___ *No* ___

Giving a true opinion?

Yes ___ *No* ___

Elaborating or clarifying ideas through examples or analogies?

Yes ___ *No* ___

Summarizing everyone's ideas?

Yes ___ *No* ___

Can they successfully:

Maintain positive relations with others?

Yes ___ *No* ___

Encourage the contributions of others?

Yes ___ *No* ___

Set the standard for positive expressions?

Yes ___ *No* ___

Facilitate the contributions of others by ensuring equitable talking time?

Yes ___ *No* ___

Summarize the group's feelings and reactions?

Yes ___ *No* ___

Do they avoid antiteam bullying behaviors such as:

Aggressively criticizing to deflate the status of others?

Yes ___ *No* ___

Blocking progress by rejecting all new ideas?

Yes ___ *No* ___

Seeking excessive recognition by talking loudly or interrupting others?

Yes ___ *No* ___

Cutting off other speakers to block their flow of ideas?

Yes ___ *No* ___

Any no answer compels the manager to address the item with her reports.

THE FIVE STAGES OF TEAM DEVELOPMENT

Every manager needs to be aware of the behaviors that help develop a team so that he can manage and lead in an exemplary manner. In research conducted with physician leaders in the Physician Executive MBA program at the University of Tennessee, five distinct stages of team development were identified: novel politeness, goal clarity, vying for voice, constructive communication, and collaboration.[4] Within these stages are the management and leadership skills designed to replace the antiteam bullying behaviors. We have refined these stages over the years in our attempts to help executives develop leadership teams for their organizations.

Stage 1: Novel Politeness

This stage of the team process has more to do with self-orientation than with teamwork. It is characterized by the following behavior: tentative, reserved, measuring each other as they search for information about each other, learning about and from each other, confusion and frustration in communication, and experiencing self-doubt along with growing self-confidence. A group begins to form only when feedback from each other and from management about performance is introduced in the process.

Stage 2: Goal Clarity

During this second stage the attention of each member of the group shifts from a self-orientation to an external objective. Only with feedback that demonstrates the gap between the observed performance of the members and the expected performance does the team transition. When the challenge of the goal is clear and the criteria for the kind of and degree of learning necessary is also clear, the group begins to orient itself to the task at hand. The second stage is still one of orientation, but the difference is that the group has received the direction to success. Soon after this group realization, when the energy of the team has been focused, a third stage emerges.

Stage 3: Vying for Voice

When the energies of the members of the group begin to move in the same direction, there are also likely to be some exchanges among members that can be called by another name—conflict. Conflict results from different agendas and ways of doing things. There will undoubtedly be bids for power over the group and within the group. In this third stage, adversity and diversity in thought and action emerge as often as persuasion and provocation.

This third stage is the greatest challenge for the group. But conflict is normal, and dealing with it successfully helps the group bond into a team. The group must persevere through this stage if it is ever to become a team. The convergence of individually based norms of behavior that are centered on self-interest has to be reconciled with the more universally accepted norms of behavior that ensure fairness and equal dignity to each person.

This stage never goes away completely as the team development process continues. Vying for voice is key to the success of the team. It adds integrity to the team process because each team member can express his or her opinion. Depending on the level of resolution of the conflict between self-interest norms and universal norms in different areas of concern, members usually report different outcomes. Not surprisingly, better communication, greater respect, and sharing of information occur when a greater number of team members have reached consensus on the direction of the action to be taken.

Stage 4: Constructive Communication

In this stage true team behavior is exhibited. Individual egos are still active, but in greater awareness of a common mission. Here every individual can contribute, will be listened to irrespective of the intensity or diversity of her voice, and the problem will be worked through until a majority has reached a consensus. Working through the problem ensures optimal learning about the problem itself. As this becomes more characteristic of a team, there emerge real moments of synergy.

Stage 5: Synergistic Collaboration

This fifth stage may not actually be a stage at all as reports indicate that it comes and goes seemingly on its own. The longevity or brevity of this stage is not dependent on individual behavior but on the synchronicity of a team's behavior. In fact, one team member has remarked that the harder you try to maintain it, the faster you lose it.

It is interesting to note that reports of this kind of experience occurred more in subteams than in large teams of 20 or more. When it is present, it speaks to a team's overall discipline, determination, and dedication to making the best decisions that can be made—and not any individual behavior or series of individual behaviors.

Summary

- **Novel politeness (requires management):** Team members are tentative, measured, and confused, and they experience some self-doubt. This has more to do with self-orientation, but it is necessary for team development.

- **Goal clarity (requires management):** There is a shift to an external objective that is clear in its expectation.

- **Vying for voice (requires leadership):** Conflict occurs as differences in thinking, planning, doing, and leading emerge.

- **Constructive communication (requires management and leadership):** Team members practice listening and empathy, and they move toward consensus collaboratively.

- **Synergistic collaboration (requires leadership):** Power is shared so as to get things done, and this stage is characterized by emotional strength and good ego management. Also, there is an effortless process in which there is discipline, determination, and dedication to the team and its task.

With good management and leadership practices in place, if bullying emerges, the manager, confident that he has fulfilled his responsibilities, can address it effectively. First, the manager will document critical incidents in order to identify what type of bully he is dealing with, and then he will develop a script based on the critical incidents.

BULLIES ON THE COUCH: KNOW THE BULLIES BETTER THAN THEY KNOW THEMSELVES

With ignorance comes fear—from fear comes bigotry.
Education is the key to acceptance.
—KATHLEEN PATEL, *The Bullying Epidemic*[5]

We all have the instinct for survival. It is part of our psychological makeup. This survival instinct can cause us to be impatient, devious, controlling, self-absorbed, self-adoring, and lacking in self-discipline and impulse control. These behaviors are the same behaviors that are manifest in the four types of bullies—except that bullies have taken it to an extreme, targeting others and causing them emotional, mental, or physical harm.

Almost all of us:

- Have bullied another person, sibling, friend, peer, or someone else at some point in our lives in one of the four ways.

- Have passed along half-truths.

- Have blocked someone from contributing her ideas.

- Have been instinctively inappropriate in our interpersonal exchanges.

- Have maneuvered the attention of the conversation back to ourselves.

- Have been overly forceful, rolling over another person and his ideas.

If these behaviors are infrequent incidents, even though not ideal, they are not bullying per se. If the incidents become exacerbated, fester, and become chronically routine with the purpose of demeaning and devaluing another and decreasing that person's productivity or success on the team, it becomes bullying. We all have a responsibility not to become a bully. Once we have owned that responsibility and accepted that we have to monitor ourselves, we can recognize the natural human tendency to grow and develop. Focusing on this tendency allows our personal worth and self-confidence to increase with each positive accomplishment.

THE NATURAL HUMAN TENDENCY TO GROW

Many thought leaders in the world of psychology have crafted their own words to depict this natural human tendency to grow.[6]

J. P. Piaget (1973) described it as an "active mind seeking knowledge."

Sigmund Freud (1917) represented it as the convergence of three growth forces: instinct, morality, and reason.

Carl Jung (1964) called it the "lifelong quest for meaning."

Eric Fromm (1941) defined it as the freedom to be productive.

Carl Rogers (1959) characterized it as a tendency to be a fully functioning personality.

Karen Horney (1950) identified it as an inner force common in all human beings.

Kurt Lewin (1947) referred to it as the "expansion of personal life space."

Edgar H. Schein advocated for humble leadership to create a fully functioning corporate culture in which quality, productivity, safety, and employee morale are optimized because individuals are allowed to use their human tendency to grow by being curious and genuinely interested in the other person.[7] Bullies squash this natural human tendency to grow and develop in their targets— as well as in the corporate culture of an organization.

Bullies mask their fears with disorderly behaviors meant to cover up their insecurities and jealousies, thus denying themselves a chance to grow and develop. They harbor fears of failure, rejection, being wrong, being weak, being ignored, not being able to change fast enough; feelings of inferiority, insecurity, or being an imposter; jealousy, extreme fear of being vulnerable and loss of control; or traumatic, emotionally significant past experiences. They may be projecting their differences in values, beliefs, or unconscious biases.

Bullies may be acting from any number of other root causes: a lack of training in how to get along with people without crossing boundaries; anxiety about a difficult task; an unseen power struggle with someone in the company; unmet personal expectations; a general state of rebellion; different manners and etiquette learned from family patterns; self-consciousness about their accents and language differences; or a host of other personal problems and stressors. It also may be because they lack other skills, such as delegation, decision-making, communication, problem solving, resilience, and endurance.

These are not excuses for the bully. Knowing this kind of information about someone on your team who is bullying others is valuable as you, the manager, can bring in a coach to help with either training or coaching.

Bullying behavior starts in the mind of the bully as a negative emotion. If it is not properly processed by the person there and then, it can fester into a mental judgment about someone. This is targeting. Once a target has been identified, the bully will begin to process justifications for projecting that negativity onto the person. The bully's mind is then mostly closed to any value the target may or may not bring to work. Bullying behavior soon appears. It is a negative emotion projected, usually aggressively, onto others without true justification. Often the bully has created false evidence in his own mind that he has accepted as truth. Once that happens, not only does bullying behavior emerge but it becomes very difficult to reset the relationship.

YOUR CHOICE

No one can make you feel inferior without your consent.
—ELEANOR ROOSEVELT

We all have fears. Fear triggers anxiety. We all experience anxiety. Anxiety triggers our survival instinct, causing us to experience a fight, flight, or freeze modality. If we allow ourselves to be dependent when we are being bullied, we may acquiesce to the bully and not stand up for ourselves. If we choose to flee the scene of bullying, which many of us opt to do, we carry the stress of that experience with us to the next scene. If you choose to fight, this book is invaluable to you.

We also have a list of seminars in the Appendix that we suggest using to back up coaching. As coaches, we try to help bullies identify the underlying causes for their aberrant behavior. Often the boss of the bully is involved in the coaching. The bullies need training on how to use both management and leadership in their style, and they must gain an understanding of the use of power, influence, empathy, and resilience, as well as dialogue and communication skills. When bullies resist development in these areas, they usually derail their career because of their need for immediate gratification, inability to accept feedback or coaching, and unwillingness to look within themselves.

For those who choose the natural tendency toward growth as managers and leaders, it begins with having patience in their own development, learning how to self-reflect, being willing to accept feedback and coaching, and choosing to invest in themselves by developing positive relations with others.

> *What seems to be of the utmost importance to humans is how we feel about who we are. We long to look good in the eyes of others, to feel good about ourselves, to be worthy of others' care and attention. We share a longing for dignity—the feeling of inherent value and worth.*
> —Donna Hicks,
> *Dignity: Its Essential Role in Resolving Conflict*

POSITIVE TEAM BEHAVIORS VERSUS THE TOXIC BEHAVIORS OF THE SOCIOPATH ON THE TEAM

There are two ways managers can deal with the sociopath on the team in order to create a positive team environment. First, they can decrease and eliminate the toxic, antiteam behaviors and replace them with team-building behaviors. Second, they can increase task and relationship synergistic team practices. We have already shared suggestions for engaging a bully one-on-one. Now we will focus on team skills.[8]

The nonfunctional, toxic behavior by either the manager or members of the team that do not help create a team environment include the following:

- Aggressively criticizing, being hostile, or deflating others' sense of worth

- Blocking progress by rejecting all ideas; arguing and controlling too much

- Confessing personal feelings about non-group-related issues

- Competing for attention by talking too much so as to be seen as the best

- Soliciting sympathy for one's own situation, problems, or misfortunes

- Seeking recognition by excessive, loud talking about extreme ideas

- Seeking special attention for pet concerns or philosophies

- Disrupting progress by joking, mimicking, or teasing others

- Disengaging by doodling, whispering, or daydreaming

- Spreading false rumors and naysaying after a meeting

- Cutting off speakers

- Constantly changing focus by wandering off topic

These behaviors slow down and prevent a group from becoming a team. They need to be eliminated and replaced with the following team-building task behaviors. On a high-performing team, the responsibilities of management and leadership can be shared with all members of the team.

Team-Building Skills

- Comparing decisions and accomplishments against group goals

- Analyzing, discerning, and determining main blocks to progress

- Taking measured steps to eliminate difficulties preventing progress

- Testing consensus by asking for individual and group opinions

- Harmonizing and conciliating differences of opinion in public

- Mediating for compromised solutions and steps forward

Task Skills

- Initiating new ideas and new ways to reframe a problem to solve it

- Seeking information and additional facts for clarification

- Soliciting opinions, feelings, or clarifications of values

- Sharing information, facts, illustrations, and examples to help clarify

- Offering an opinion, a belief, a suggestion, or a value

- Elaborating on or clarifying a task

- Showing a coordinated relationship among various tasks and ideas

- Summarizing everyone's ideas and suggestions by vocalizing them

People Skills

- Encouraging the contributions of others with praise and civil responses

- Setting a standard for positive individual expressions and group decisions

- Responding with positive regard to the good ideas of others as they emerge

- Facilitating the contributions of others by ensuring equivalent talking time

- Summarizing the group's feelings and reactions to ideas proposed

- Relieving tension by using humor to dispel negative feelings

- Relieving tension by presenting the situation in a wider context

FOSTERING TEAMWORK

Coming together is a beginning; keeping together is progress; working together is success.
—HENRY FORD

Teams are an integral part of an organization. Teams fail to develop when there is little trust, fear of speaking much less confronting, a tendency to avoid conflict, low levels of patience, too much control of contributions, and little to no feedback on the impact of interpersonal exchanges. These conditions foster bullying in the workplace.

The benefits of a positive team environment are many. When individuals on a team are encouraged to examine opposing viewpoints, they often find themselves challenged to defend their ideas. Working through this type of controlled conflict in an atmosphere of trust can transform rivals competing with each other to rivals acting on their best knowledge and know-how in synergistic collaboration. As problems are solved by the group, the result is work that has been fully considered and, in essence, pretested through greater disclosure, feedback, listening, and loyalty by every member of the team. As economist, management guru, and author Peter Drucker said, "No executive has ever suffered because his subordinates were strong and effective."

BOSSES WHO BULLY ARE DISENGAGING PEOPLE FROM THEIR WORK

According to a 2013 report by Gallup, there are three categories of engagement: *fully engaged*, in which workers are positively and emotionally connected to the work, are energetic, are productive, and have good working relations with their managers; *not engaged*, in which workers do not invest emotional energy in their work and more or less sleepwalking through the workday; and *actively disengaged*, in which workers are using their energy for everything else but accomplishment of work or just complying to avoid punishment.[9]

In both cases, the not engaged and actively disengaged are disconnected from their work, and their full attentive powers are dampened. Although there may be many reasons for this unproductive situation, there is often one common reason: the workers' relationship with the manager. If the manager is a bully, this often results in a loss of productivity and workers becoming actively disengaged or not engaged at all if they can get away with it. The Gallup report suggests that up to 70 percent of American workers are not engaged or actively disengaged. Even though there may be other contributing factors, we know from our coaching and consulting experience that the cause is often a negative relationship with a bully manager.

Moreover, with the move from hierarchical company structures to flatter, globally distributed networks where the work is customized, requiring greater communication and collaboration, and with the increase of generation X and millennials in the workforce who desire to work anytime and anywhere, crafting their own work output, we see the increase in bullying behavior as the last-ditch attempt by traditionalists and baby boomers to control the changes at work. The workplace itself is in transition.

As Jacob Morgan suggests in his book *The Future of Work*, employment and management are fundamentally changing in the direction of manager-less companies.[10] The employees want to have the potential to become leaders in their work, as everyone now can be leaders even without a managerial title. It is almost as if bosses are at a crossroads. They can adapt or bully. The managers who are adaptable will learn to lead by example and use control only as a last resort. Others will cling to direct or indirect bullying behavior, refusing to leave the bunker from which they believe they can control the workplace.

AVOIDING LITTLE DEATHS EVERY DAY

When up to 60 percent of our adult lives are spent at work, we are inclined naturally to want to get better and better at what we do.

Usually, we want to be given the freedom to perform at our best without the obstacles of managerial control or bullying behavior.

Human beings have a natural tendency and a productive capacity to grow, to develop, and to accomplish good works, and we all tend to gravitate toward opportunities in which we have the room and encouragement to grow.

Not being able to fulfill our potential and feeling that our growth is being held back because we are being bullied is like experiencing little deaths each day. Work should be purposeful for the company and meaningful for the individual, and it should support the natural human tendency to grow and develop.

CREATING A BULLY-PROOF WORKPLACE

Cooperation is the thorough conviction that nobody can get there unless everybody gets there.
—Victoria Burden,
The Process of Intuition

For Jonathan Martin, the 2013 Bullygate scandal resulted in his leaving the Miami Dolphins. For Richie Incognito, it culminated in his suspension for conduct detrimental to the team until 2014. He later admitted in an interview with Jay Glazer on *Fox NFL Sunday*, "I have been like a cancer in the locker rooms. . . . I have been selfish. I haven't been a good teammate. I have made plenty of mistakes: mistakes I have learned from, mistakes that have changed me, mistakes that have made me realize I need to get help. I have sought counseling; I've made changes in my personal life. I've done the steps necessary to grow."

For us, the lesson of the Martin and Incognito story was a wake-up call. Who would have thought that football players could be bullied? But this story is not about who was right and who was wrong or how sincere or insincere either one of them was. Nor is it about what the NFL did or did not do. Rather, Bullygate is about how important it is to recognize how we treat each other at work and about the need to create a bully-proof workplace. As executive coaches for more than 30 years, we have witnessed the negative impact of a bully in an organization. We know that changing the culture of a company or team is hard to do and that it takes time—but it can be done through cooperation and collaboration. The result is a workplace that is productive, engaged, and happy, which translates to a healthier bottom line.

A bully-proof workplace is one where all workers are fully engaged and committed to getting work done while maintaining positive relations with all stakeholders in the company. Employees feel like owners. The leaders stand willing and able to do what they must to ensure the workers' success. The workers in turn communicate honestly and openly with colleagues, reports, peers, and bosses. Leaders engage with employees. Together, they build trust and integrity. The relationships are reciprocal, and responsibility is shared between worker and leader.

The secret to a bully-proof workplace is effective communication. In this day and age, when we have so many channels through which we communicate, it is relatively easy to disseminate the expectations for a bully-proof workplace to employees in a timely fashion. In the following section of this chapter, we provide a sample of a Bully-Proof Workplace Policy Statement that clarifies the expectations in behavior. That is followed by "The 10 Tenets of a Bully-Proof Workplace," which we recommend be customized and used for an employee-wide training program. The goal is that everyone on every level know how to stand up for himself or herself when dealing with a bully and to do so in a clear, respectful, and authentic manner. A workplace is bully-proof when anyone can step into the arena and lead on a topic, an issue, or a concern without fear of threat, suspicion, or mistreatment.

SAMPLE POLICY STATEMENT FOR A BULLY-PROOF WORKPLACE

We, the Board of Directors, executive leadership, management, and all employed at _____ are committed to a bully-proof workplace where all people, regardless of race, gender, background, belief system, or position in the company, are treated with respect, dignity, and civility. Any type of bullying that demeans, diminishes, defames, or belittles a person through rumor, lies, devious and selfish acts, boastful and derogatory comments toward others, antisocial or aggressive behavior, or any acts that create a hostile work environment for a person or persons who have been repeatedly targeted in a consistent manner will not be tolerated. If this behavior is identified, corrective action will be taken immediately to realign the bully with the 10 tenets espoused by the company for a bully-proof workplace included in this policy statement. If the first corrective action is not successful, the secondary response will follow with standard performance management protocols used by the company.

Date: _____

Printed name: _____

Signature: _____

THE 10 TENETS FOR A BULLY-PROOF WORKPLACE

The 10 tenets were derived from our experience as executive coaches. While working with executives, we discerned recurring patterns of behavior that were and were not acceptable or supportive for productivity. These patterns were formulated into positively phrased tenets supporting a bully-proof workplace.

1. Act and Speak with Integrity, Honesty, Sincerity, Fairness—and Always Keep Your Word

The most exhausting thing in life is being insincere.
—ANNE MORROW LINDBERGH

Establish integrity in the organization as the foundation upon which a bully-proof workplace is built. This action will cultivate the development of character in all employees, directing constant attention to the choices made at work when dealing with each other. When these choices become habituated into long-lasting behaviors, they help bring about a bully-proof workplace that honors honesty, sincerity, fairness, and promise keeping and avoids any and all bullying or coercive tactics.

Bringing honesty and sincerity into communication builds trust. Behaviors to practice include these:

- Not repeating false statements and spreading rumors

- Acting with the expectation that each exchange is one of many more to come

- Acting with the intent of building a long-term relationship

- Avoiding conflict-of-interest relationships

- Allowing others to speak and listening to them

- Sharing and giving credit for good work

- Showing respect in times of stress

- Honoring all promises, commitments, and contracts

- Respecting the intrinsic worth and dignity of all

- Resolving conflicts with honesty and open discussion, not coercion

2. Practice Courage with Sound Judgment and Self-Control

Moral excellence comes about as a result of habit.
We become just by doing just acts, temperate by doing
temperate acts, brave by doing brave acts.
—ARISTOTLE

Courage is practiced by recognizing and pursuing the right way to make a good decision and discerning the difference between what is appropriately helpful and what is potentially harmful in the process. It is having the strength of mind to stay on the right course of action despite adversity in the forms of criticism, skepticism, sarcasm, and lack of enthusiasm by others. It is practicing self-discipline, self-restraint, and self-editing of all unruly impulses and reactions. It is choosing moderation, delaying gratification, and controlling anger and frustration.

Behaviors to practice include these:

- Resisting impulsive, angry, and reactive behavior

- Controlling your ego

- Monitoring your area of responsibility so you can make good judgments for the company

- Exhibiting prudence and temperance so your decisions are based on comprehensiveness and patience, not insecurities and inadequacies

- Exercising careful judgment in the use of your expertise and power at work

- Being aware of the potential conflict between people's rights and task duties

3. Stay Aware of Your Impact in Interpersonal Interactions

The deepest principle in human nature is the craving to be appreciated.
—WILLIAM JAMES

Honor human decency and the rights and dignity of others, especially those who are different, by displaying mutual respect, openness, patience, kindness, generosity, politeness, and compassion. Refrain from interrupting others in midsentence; be sensitive to their perception of their personal worth in the workplace; and cause no harm. Members of a bully-proof workplace are able to differentiate how they feel about themselves and how they relate to others as distinct from how others feel within themselves and how they relate to others. Give and receive information and feedback respectfully to better understand the needs of others. A lack of this awareness between your needs and the needs of others will have a negative effect in conversations and on overall productivity.

Delivering difficult feedback is not easy. It requires nondefensive listening, empathy, and a sensitivity to others, as well as the skill to self-monitor how the interaction is going in real time. The person giving feedback needs to ensure that the delivery of the message is without bias, premature judgment, or admonishment using a harsh tone of voice. Engage respectfully in dialogue without creating fear, and give the other person the feeling that his personal worth has been retained. To do this, focus your full attention on the other while keeping at bay any preconceived perceptions and expectations that limit your intake of that person's message. The other person will experience what being heard feels like—acceptance—which will draw him even more into the conversation. He can then better use the information and feedback for improvement.

When receiving information and feedback, one can summarize the information in the exchange and paraphrase back one's understanding of what the other person has said to reach a joint understanding. This encourages and reaffirms that the exchange has a sense of fair play.

Other suggestions include these:

- Making it effortless for the other person to offer constructive feedback

- Making it comfortable for the other person to critique the work process

- Making it safe for the other person to complain about bullying

- Demonstrating in your actions that bullying is not tolerated at work

- Showing that the feedback or complaint is appreciated and will be responded to within a certain span of time, such as within the next 48 hours, if possible

- Taking suggestions on how to improve the culture

4. Practice Nondefensive Listening

Listening builds strength in other people.
—Robert Greenleaf[1]

To focus your attention on what another is really saying to gain complete understanding requires the self-monitoring technique of nondefensive listening. This happens by reducing the number of times there are interruptions in your own thinking with random and unrelated thoughts and by suppressing the temptation to form your own defensive responses to what is being said, all of which prevents effective listening. This requires self-restraint, honesty, and a willingness to hear the truth.

The results of nondefensive listening are more dialoguing (a give-and-take in conversation) among members and not telling or demanding; dialoguing to reach agreement on a joint understanding; purposeful intent to gain multiple perspectives; and more disclosure of information in the exchanges. Conversations will stay on message; people will be able to communicate their whole message, and they can pause to think in conversations because they lack fear.

The practice of nondefensive listening requires the following:

- Patience and acceptance to put the speaker at ease

- The removal of distractions, both inner and external

- The occasional clarifying of the message with questions such as "May we pause to make sure I understood what has been said so far?" and "Please help me know more about . . ."

- Encouraging speakers that their message is important by repeating the words they used, using affirming statements such as "I see," and maintaining good eye contact

- Appreciating the message with comments such as "This is good to know. What other aspects are involved?"

- Suspending judgment by focusing on the worth of the content

- Asking more questions and not overtalking

- Summarizing the message you heard to ensure understanding

Nondefensive listening results in learning. In fact, listening can often be more informative than talking because you can hear what is *not* being said in the exchange. In today's rapidly changing workplace, listening takes on even greater importance than just gaining content knowledge. Listen not for the information you can use to back up your preexisting opinion of another person. Listen to empathize, attend, and truly understand the other.

Nondefensive listening means making an honest attempt to hear what is being said and to understand it comprehensively—that is, verbally, vocally, and visually. If we listen only to words, we may miss the fact that perhaps the sender's visual message contradicts the verbal message. For example, if the words convey a happy message and the facial expression of the sender is a frown, it is good to realize that important information may be missing in the situation. The sender's tone of voice (loud or yelling) may obscure the words, even though the verbal (the words) and visual (facial expressions) aspects signal something different. The verbal, vocal, and visual components of a message should be considered when one is giving information as well as when one is receiving information.

To be a better listener, a person can confirm what is being said by asking short questions, such as, "As I understand so far . . ." "Do you mean this . . ." and "Let me be sure I am following what you are saying." These short statements can keep the communication on track.

Nondefensive listening is rare in the workplace today. Even though most people believe they listen, they are not listening with real understanding. Yet it is one of the most potent forces for change that is known to the human race.[2]

A memorable example of the value of listening was demonstrated when Sperry Corporation and Burroughs merged into what is now known as the Unisys Corporation. There were some internal conflicts early on, before the merger was made final, because the Sperry side strongly practiced good listening skills, whereas communications at Burroughs were more variable. This conflict delayed the melding of the two organizations into one corporation. It was determined that of the four key workplace skills (speaking, reading, writing, and listening), listening was the least taught. Yet J. Paul Lyet, Sperry's chairman and CEO, strongly believed that listening should be part of the culture of the new organization, and therefore he launched a corporate policy campaign to promote listening skills years before the merger. Accordingly, Burroughs's executives and managers were encouraged to improve their practice of listening so that its employees would merge more effectively with Sperry and excel.

5. Practice Empathy with Others

If you can't determine right from wrong,
then you lack empathy, not religion.
—ANONYMOUS

The nondefensive listener, having the self-restraint to avoid unrelated thoughts and suppress her own defensiveness, has created space in the exchange to be able to practice empathy to better understand where the other person is coming from. Empathy is aligning your feelings *with* the other person, not feeling sympathy for the other person. Sympathy sends the message to the other person that he is helpless, which may diminish the potential value of the communication. Empathy helps create a sense of openness and acceptance of the thinking and feelings of the other and keeps us from evaluating and judging that person. Empathy allows you to attend carefully to the other person and hear what he *says* and *needs*.

Practicing empathy is evidenced by signs of encouragement from the listener that include verbal ("I see," "Tell me more about that," and so on) and visual cues (eye contact, nodding, and avoiding other visual distractions, such as cell phones and computers, during the exchange). The choice to practice empathy with others is the basis for ego management and development of emotional strength.

6. Develop Your Emotional Strength Through Ego Management

Self-command is the main elegance.
—RALPH WALDO EMERSON

Ego is the inner self. Ego development begins at birth, and it is socialized, educated, and influenced by a myriad of different experiences and events through adulthood.

An ego can be healthy or unhealthy. Understanding the place ego has in self-development allows an individual to examine and manage her own expectations and direction. It is important to learn that ego management is the continual conversation we have between the inner self and the outer self to ensure that we are not excluding others in our deliberations. This helps maintain a healthy ego.

If a person's ego is big and unhealthy and drives him to think and act only for himself, there is little room for empathy. Reining in or suppressing ego surges so that the ego can remain in a healthy state requires a balance between ego and empathy. The results of practicing empathy are sharing accomplishments among all stakeholders and engaging in dialogue without fear, slights, demeaning behavior, and bullying. People need to use their personal power to communicate and not to intimidate.

The ability to manage one's ego and to keep it healthy is fundamental to being a boss. Being able to manage oneself inwardly is the key to managing and leading outwardly. The capacity to monitor ego, manage ego, and manage functions (that is, selecting, organizing, directing, and controlling) can be most successful when decisions are based on unselfish needs. This learning comes about from the recognition of the vital importance of using empathy with others to help manage and monitor the ego.

Individuals with healthy egos are open to continuous self-development. The healthy ego faces fear and bravely chooses the best path forward. The development of a healthy ego is not characterized by egotism, fear of being seen as an imposter, fear of rejection, anger, aggressiveness, or narcissism. Rather, it is a healthy ego that calls upon the better side of our natures for our interactions with others.

Healthy egos guide individuals to embrace humility. Humility is the ability to put others first and admit when you are wrong. It inspires others dealing with the challenges of volatility, uncertainty, complexity, and ambiguity at work. Humility can bring out the best in everyone and release positive energy throughout an organization.

7. Recognize and Deal Effectively with the Emotions of Others

> *When we put ourselves in the other person's place,*
> *we're less likely to want to put him in his place.*
> —*Farmer's Digest*

Rapid change and heavy workloads can tax our emotions. Understanding the emotional base from which a person is speaking helps one empathize with that person and offers the opportunity to grasp the context as well as the content of another's message. It is easier to respond to issues and act like a professional when you are able to see the situation through the other person's emotions. When their emotions have calmed and the issue is resolved, she will remember the patience, selflessness, and fair play you demonstrated in the conversation.

We've all had the experience of someone's unloading his emotions on us at some point in our careers. Those emotions may range from anger, sadness, and fear to surprise, shame, and disgust. Whenever such emotions are directed toward you, two things are happening: your ego drives you to a decision to either fight or flee, or to pursue a road to resolution—depending on whether your ego is a healthy one. The wise way is to deal with the emotions first and then deal with the context and content of the issue.

Think of a person you know in your workplace who you feel does not always act professionally. Now, instead of feeling your own emotions, focus your attention on why the other person may be acting that way. Try to see it from her point of view. Dwell on that point of view for a few minutes. Chances are that from this moment onward, you will have less of an emotional response and more of a mindful one to the person. That is the power of listening and ego management. Reflect back the emotion to reduce it by saying, "Help me understand why you are so concerned about this."

Once the other person has recognized his emotion because you have reflected it back to him, it can, and usually does, help him gain control over it. By acknowledging it directly with one of the above questions, you can proceed to communicate your understanding of the other person's problem without judgment, scorn, or anger. Once the emotion is no longer in the pathway of communication, you can probe more deeply into its cause. When you act to resolve the concern of someone else, you can help him move on to the real issues.

8. Practice and Monitor Your Use of Personal and Position Power

What lies in our power to do, it lies in our power not to do.
—Aristotle

Power is present in all parts of the dynamic of every human interaction, and it needs to be balanced. Current workplace configurations such as global and interdependent jobs, job sharing, and virtual jobs require a prudent use of personal and position power in which the focus is on others in the company.

When we practice our personal power using nondefensive listening, empathy, and keeping the focus of the exchange on a balanced give-and-take in the interaction, it often helps others in *their* work. We often see that when a person is using nondefensive and nonjudgmental listening, empathy, and the guiding principles of integrity, she is looked up to by others as having potential for leadership. Others realize that the person is not out for herself, so the trust level goes up. If praised for this, she has to be careful *not* to inflate her self-importance and lessen her impulse control. The behavior may start to move in the direction of bullying behavior if the praise goes to her head and her ego goes awry.

Without proper preparation in dealing with this increase of feeling more powerful, two unfortunate results may occur. First, people who feel more powerful, either because they received praise from others or because they have discerned that others are deferring to them with more attention, can drive for ego domination over others. That false impression of self-importance is further reinforced when they are surrounded by sycophantic employees who believe that to safeguard their job, it is safer to reinforce the selfish and aggressive behavior they witness. Meanwhile, because the feeling of being powerful has the propensity to escalate self-importance, they have no time or tolerance for the fruitful practices of integrity (openness, generosity, patience, and civility) and interpersonal communication skills (ego management, listening, empathy, and polite give-and-take).

If people are feeling personally powerful and now have position power, it is extremely important to be diligent not to corrupt their personal power. And the people feeling personally powerful would be wise to practice the following:

- Recognize that positive leadership consists of using a balance of personal power and position power, which increases productivity as a result.

- Treat all work colleagues with consideration and respect and be alert to anyone on the team who may be using oppressive tactics to get work done.

- Deal with people in a way that uplifts, inspires, and supports.

- Understand the issues of age, gender, or race that play into communication.

- Observe the formal and informal structures of communication in the organization.

9. Stand Up to Bullying with Positive Resolve

It is not the strongest of the species that survive,
but the one most responsive to change.
—CHARLES DARWIN

A person-centered, nonauthoritarian, bully-proof workplace, in which people are sensitive to the dynamics of power among all stakeholders and do not mislead or exploit others, is created one conversation at a time, using genuine, ethical communication. Genuine communication requires fairness, respect, and courage. It has the power to dismantle bullying by creating an open and honest work atmosphere.[3]

Stand up to bullying by documenting critical incidents of bullying behavior, using prepared scripts for dealing with each type of bully, and taking an everyday approach of being proactive before conflict arises. That includes bringing into everyday conversations factual information, self-awareness, and the 10 tenets; responding in conversation in a way that creates a climate of zero tolerance of bullying; being vigilant in every conversation to increase a positive attitude toward creating a bully-proof workplace; and practicing uplifting comments in all conversations. For example, look for the silver-lining benefit to the company and use it as a teachable moment instead of blaming a person for a downturn in business. The consequences of these practices create pride in your people that they are part of something important, are continuously learning, have a sense of ownership, and enjoy being nice at work.

10. Model Effective Human Relations Skills

Employees are most enthusiastic when they can work collaboratively with others in a workplace free of threat and suspicion.
—DALTON KEHOE

Antiteam behaviors slow down and prevent a group from becoming a team and need to be eliminated in the workplace or they will derail a positive team environment and a bully-proof workplace.

Replace antiteam behaviors with team-building practices such as these:

- Dealing with difficulties in a measured way by getting others' opinions out on the table

- Patiently pursuing decisions by using proper comparisons, good analysis, and discernment

- Harmonizing any differences with compromise and judgment moving forward

Other behaviors that help complete tasks on time include these:

- Seeking information and opinions from others

- Sharing information and opinions for greater clarification

- Elaborating and summarizing tasks at work that help future planning

Positive people skills help create a good team environment and a bully-proof workplace. These include the following:

- Encouraging others to speak at meetings

- Facilitating the flow of information and everyone's involvement

- Setting the standard for proper and appropriate interaction among members

IMAGINE YOUR JOB IN A BULLY-PROOF WORKPLACE

Imagine a good night's sleep without obsessing about an exchange in front of others with a coworker who slighted your ability to do your job.

Imagine that when you first wake up in the morning to get ready for work, you happily begin to think of completing with efficiency and effectiveness the tasks, meetings, planning sessions, and one-on-one conversations that you have on your agenda. Even though you will be interacting with people at work who are above you in rank, of equal rank to you, and subordinate to you, there should be no difference in the way you interact with them.

Imagine that you have power *with* others and not over others. The goal is to be as productive as possible and accomplish as much as possible without wasting time, energy, or resources. You know your colleagues at work will support you if and when you need their thoughts, suggestions, or expertise, because you have trusting working relationships with everyone.

Imagine that when deadlines loom, the environment becomes even more consciously supportive, helpful, and kind. When there is no deadline looming, you notice that people don't waste their time being idle and instead look for whatever else needs to get done.

Imagine that there is always a feeling of continuous improvement occurring along with a shared commitment to addressing the constant change and disruptions of a company operating in a global environment.

EPILOGUE

Right is right, even if everyone is against it;
wrong is wrong, even if everyone is for it.
—WILLIAM PENN

The information provided in this book shows you how to stop the workplace from becoming a breeding ground for bullies and how to address it in a comprehensive way.

As coaches, we encourage and help facilitate the growth, development, and prosperity of our clients. We want our clients to win *with others* at work without lying, manipulating, grandstanding, or rolling over others to do well and move up in their companies. We are always saddened by executives who truly believe that the way to power is through use of force, manipulation, and hidden agendas. The irony for us is that when we work with these clients, we usually discover that they have been bullied at some point in their careers. Many bullies are repeating the bullying behavior they were exposed to in the past, and they use that past experience to justify their behavior.

Given the consequences of bullying, it is our strong belief that any form of bullying is *not* good management or good leadership, even though a bully might believe he is a good manager or leader. Bullying is the misuse and/or abuse of power. It crushes potential output in terms of productivity, comprehensive reasoning, informed judgment, and the desire to accomplish goals that will cause a positive outcome in the company or in the world. Bullying destroys employee growth and costs the company a fortune while simultaneously weakening the mission and vision of the organization. Most people, usually under stress, will exhibit bullying behavior from time to time. We are human, after all, but a committed bully exhibits the behavior almost all the time. You don't have to go far to encounter bullying, whether as a target or as a bystander. The question is, will we muster the courage and words to confront it?

Bullying is not a gender issue. It is an issue of the abuse and/or misuse of power. Also, it is a lack of interpersonal competence on the bully's part and a lack of understanding of how to deal with bullying on the target's part. Bullying is everywhere, not just in the workplace. It is a widespread issue, and we want this book to be a clarion call to all who care to focus their attention on how we treat each other. Wherever bullying occurs, there are ways to confront it, ameliorate it, and transform our interpersonal interactions with others into more respectful communication. We hope this book is a meaningful contribution toward establishing a more ideal and civil society.

We offer one last story that continues to inspire us. The setting for this true story was a seminar at which executives from the workplace and veteran lower school teachers came together to strategize learning opportunities from both work settings. Executives were paired with schoolteachers for the initial activity.

In one such pairing, a Boeing executive was paired with a veteran third-grade teacher. The Boeing executive immediately began complaining as he perceived there was little he could learn from a third-grade schoolteacher, even with her 30 years of experience.

The group tolerated his complaining patiently until his learning opportunity emerged.

The Boeing executive said to the teacher, "What can you possibly know about what happens in my world at work? You are a third-grade schoolteacher."

The teacher, Cynthia, calmly replied, "We teachers know exactly what goes on in your workplace."

The executive pressed, "How could you possibly know what goes on in my workplace?"

Cynthia calmly responded, "We know what happens in your workplace through the behavior of your children."

Suddenly, this tough, aggressive, 6-foot-6-inch-tall Boeing executive had an aha moment. He immediately saw the connection, something that had never occurred to him. He followed around this diminutive third-grade teacher for the entire week-long seminar. He was trying to learn as much as he could about what she had gleaned about the workplace from her students so he could bring the information back to Boeing.

Our children internalize what they observe in our homes and the stories they hear about work at the dinner table. Our children are watching. Let us model the right behavior for them. Let us take the opportunity to make a real difference in our society by doing what we can, every day, to exemplify in our actions, words, and deeds true civility, kindness, and compassion toward others.

APPENDIX

INSTRUMENTS AND ASSESSMENTS USED IN COACHING THE 10 TENETS

DISC

Hogan Assessment Systems

Life Styles Inventory (LSI)

NEO Personality Inventory (PI-R)

Skills Assessment

A SAMPLING OF SEMINARS USED TO TRAIN FOR A BULLY-PROOF WORKPLACE

Practicing the Essentials in Business: Integrity, Etiquette, and Civility

Building Personal Resilience and Courage

Building Positive Assertive Communication Skills

Developing a Career: Getting in Touch with Your Strengths and Skills

Building Your Personal Brand in a Bully-Proof Workplace

Practicing Giving and Receiving Feedback: A Crucial Practice

Making Room for Emotional Intelligence at Work

Developing a Confident Presence in Times of Stress

Practicing the Essential Interpersonal Skills to Enhance Your Gravitas

Understanding Political Savvy to Optimize Your Influence

Managing Conflict, Confrontation, and Difficult Conversations

Strategic Networking That Builds Social Capital

Team Effectiveness: Developing a Group into a Team

Workplace Bullying: How to Create Inclusiveness at Work

DISC: THE FOUR VOICES OF INTERACTION FOR INTERPERSONAL COMPETENCE

Participants will gain insight into their leadership voices. This instrument-based session evaluates participants' capacity in the four distinct dispositions of leadership and helps them apply each of the dispositions to appropriate situations. The dispositions are the four voices within every leader to which he or she must attend when leading: people focused, task focused, control focused, and image focused.

This seminar helps participants become aware of when leaders are using their dominant voice to the disadvantage of other people's insights and ideas. Also, some of these voices are sometimes un-intentionally or unwittingly biased, whereas other voices are re-pressed in the workplace. The seminar process concludes with the recognition that openness using the four voices is critical, that we all have these four voices, and that we must exercise them at different times, depending on the situation.

OBJECTIVES

- Leaders understand the difference between buy-in and commitment.

- Leaders recognize their role in modeling the acceptance of multiple perspectives and diverse work styles.

- Leaders are able to quickly diagnose elements that are obstacles to a more inclusive culture.

- Leaders learn to develop an environment that works for all employees.

HOGAN ASSESSMENT SYSTEMS

We use the renowned Hogan Leadership Assessment Instruments that evaluate personality characteristics for success, identify factors that impede career growth, and assess business drivers and core values for individuals. The three components are the following:

1. The Hogan Personality Inventory (HPI) measures normal personality and is used to predict job performance. The HPI is a high-quality psychometric evaluation of personality characteristics that identifies the fundamental factors that distinguish personalities and determine career success.

2. The Hogan Development Survey (HDS) identifies personality-based performance risks and negatives of interpersonal behavior. These behaviors are seen most often during times of stress and may impede work relationships, hinder productivity, or limit overall career potential. Deeply ingrained in personality, these behaviors affect an individual's leadership style and actions. If these behavior patterns are recognized, however, they can be compensated for with development and coaching.

3. The Motives, Values, Preferences Inventory (MVPI) is a personality inventory that reveals a person's core values, goals, and interests. Results indicate which type of position, job, and environment will be most motivating for the employees and when they will feel the most satisfied.

LIFE STYLES INVENTORY (LSI)

Thinking styles are developed over time. The LSI tests for thinking styles that result from the sum total of experiences a person has had and how he or she interprets those experiences. The LSI measures individual thinking styles in 12 different areas of life. Some styles are constructive and positive, and others are counterproductive and linked to negative stress. The four styles at the top of the circumplex (11 o'clock to 2 o'clock) are considered constructive and stress free.

11 o'clock, Achievement: People with high scores tend to derive great satisfaction from the completion of tasks they believe to be of value, and they do so with efficiency and effectiveness.

12 o'clock, Self-Actualizing: High scores indicate a healthy self-image and high self-esteem, general satisfaction with lifestyle, and an approach to life that is confident and optimistic.

1 o'clock, Humanistic-Encouraging: High scores indicate that people are important to the person taking the assessment and that he gets a great deal of satisfaction helping others fulfill their potential. Also, high scores indicate that the person taking the assessment is sensitive and respectful to others' issues and concerns.

2 o'clock, Affiliative: High scores reflect a great interest in associating with people and spending time with them, as well as a level of commitment to forming and maintaining mutually satisfying relationships.

The remaining eight styles (3 o'clock to 10 o'clock) are considered more or less counterproductive, and high scores in each usually represent more than average levels of negative stress. Here, low scores are desirable. Thus, the coach should focus on ways to reduce the stress associated with these styles.

3 o'clock, Approval: High scores indicate that many of the person's actions are designed to gain approval from others. This can be easily translated into building equal relationships among others. The person's stress can emerge from too much focus on how others see her. Encourage the person to focus on projecting firmness of purpose and self-confidence.

4 o'clock, Conventional: High scores reflect a need to fit in or to do things by the book in an attempt to draw attention away from oneself. This stifles creativity and initiative, especially in a time of rapid change. These folks usually have significant negative stress and tend to hold on to old solutions rather than embracing new opportunities. They need to learn to balance their own convictions with the acceptance of others' belief systems.

5 o'clock, Dependent: High scores indicate excessive dependence on others' good opinions and acceptance of the person taking the assessment. This person may feel easily rejected, and he may avoid entering into relationships because he anticipates rejection. This person may feel he has little control over events and outcomes, and as a result, he may develop a passive approach. This person needs to find his own strengths and values in past accomplishments and begin to build from there.

6 o'clock, Avoidance: High scores reflect low self-esteem that could arise from dissatisfaction with career choices and/or seeing oneself as a victim of circumstances beyond one's control. Other emotions could be guilt and self-blame. This person usually needs to focus on personal and professional accomplishments and the strengths she demonstrates. She should plan her future life and career to promote self-fulfillment and avoid negative situations.

7 o'clock, Oppositional: High scores indicate a tendency to focus on dissatisfactions and express them with a negative attitude. This person is often critical, cynical, rigid, and overly sarcastic, or he has a tendency to become defensive. He can be seen as unnecessarily probing, questioning, and skeptical. Help him keep this behavior in check. Also, help him in building relationships through empathizing with others and focusing on how they feel and think.

8 o'clock, Power: High scores reflect a belief that in management or leadership, the approach based in position power is the most effective way to get people to act and cooperate. This person may overvalue the prestige and status that she gives position power, which may lead her to rely overly on control. Help her see that the real power in building relationships is based on the personal power of being aware of how others think and feel—that is, it is based on empathy, which will result in her gaining the ability to win their cooperation.

9 o'clock, Competitive: High scores indicate a preference for overly competitive situations. This environment is very stressful, and it is a counterproductive style if self-worth is too attached to winning and someone else's losing. Demonstrate to him how dangerous this is and get him to channel the energy into healthy task and relationship behaviors.

10 o'clock, Perfectionistic: High scores reflect a tendency to try to impress others by being busy and working hard, often at the expense of quality results. This person may experience frustration with herself and others when their goals are not met. This is a highly unproductive style. Help her convert that perfectionistic energy into a focus on purpose and objective—before she takes action. Help her to be more strategic.

NEO PERSONALITY INVENTORY (NEO PI-R)

The first step in interpreting a NEO PI-R profile is to examine the definitions of the five domain scales to understand personality at the broadest level. This section describes each of the domains or factors (N, E, O, A, and C), and it outlines a valuable way to use the information when coaching.

Neuroticism (N)

The N domain includes susceptibility to psychological distress when there is a general tendency to experience negative effects such as fear, sadness, embarrassment, anger, guilt, and disgust. This domain presents the contrast between emotional stability (ability to adjust) and maladjustment (neuroticism).

Men and women who score high in neuroticism experience interference in their adaptation to work by the disruptive emotions listed above. Also, it can lead to a proneness to have irrational ideas and a decreased ability to control their impulses and to cope with stress. High scores in N should *not* be viewed as a measure of psychopathology. Most of us have some percentage of neuroticism, but, one hopes, no psychoticism (delusions).

Individuals who score low in N are usually more emotionally stable. Their behavior is calm, even tempered, and relaxed. They are able to face stressful situations without becoming upset or rattled.

Extroversion (E)

There are extroverts and introverts. We believe for leaders to excel at their jobs, they need to be *ambiverts*. The facets of the E domain are warmth, gregariousness, assertiveness, activity, excitement seeking, and positive emotions.

Extroverts are sociable, assertive, active, upbeat, and energetic. They like speaking, excitement, and stimulation. They are optimistic, and they tend to be cheerful.

Introverts are more difficult to describe. They are even paced, not unhappy, and not pessimistic. They are reserved, but they may be seen by others as unfriendly. They are independent, but they may be seen by others as not being team players. They may say they are shy, but what they mean is that they prefer to work alone. They do not necessarily suffer from social anxiety. Introverts break the mental constructs that link happy versus unhappy and outgoing versus shy. Extroverts and introverts are *not* opposites. The ability to be introspective or reflective does not relate to either extroversion or introversion.

Openness to Experience (O)

The facets of the O domain are fantasy, aesthetics, feelings, actions, ideas, and values.

The elements of O include active imagination, aesthetic sensitivity, attentiveness to inner feelings, a preference for variety, intellectual curiosity, and independence of judgment.

Open individuals are curious about both inner and outer worlds in that they are willing to entertain novel ideas and unconventional values. They experience positive and negative emotions much more keenly than do closed individuals. Openness is closely related to divergent thinking and creativity.

Men and women who score low on O tend to be conventional in behavior and conservative in outlook. They prefer the familiar to the novel, and their emotional responses may be muted. These closed individuals may have a narrow band of interest, and they can be socially and/or politically conservative. Open individuals are often unconventional, they are willing to question authority, and they are prepared to entertain new ethical, social, and political ideas, but that does not mean they are unprincipled.

Openness may sound healthier than closed, or even more mature, but the value of open or closed people depends on the requirements of the situation, and both perform useful functions in society.

Agreeableness (A)

Like extroversion, agreeableness is primarily a dimension of interpersonal tendencies. The agreeable person is one who is fundamentally altruistic. He is empathetic to others and eager to help them, and he believes others will help him in return. In contrast, the disagreeable or antagonistic person is egocentric, skeptical about the intentions of others, and overly competitive (she may have a tendency to fight only for her own interests rather than being cooperative or collaborative).

Neither generally high nor low scores are intrinsically better from an individual or a social point of view. Both have value. Balance of the two poles is important. However, if the purpose is more targeted for a long-term situation, usurping one for the other might be better. For example, if the purpose is to win the war against cancer, disagreeableness is valued more than agreeableness because skeptical and critical thinking contribute to accurate analysis, especially in the sciences. Obviously, agreeable people are more popular than antagonistic people. However, extremely low A scores can be associated with the narcissistic, antisocial, and paranoid personality disorders, and extremely high A scores can be associated with the dependent personality disorder.

The facets of the A domain are straightforwardness, altruism, compliance, modesty, and tender-mindedness.

Conscientiousness (C)

The facets of the conscientiousness domain are competence, order, dutifulness, achievement and striving, self-discipline, and deliberation.

A person with high scores in conscientiousness (character) is scrupulous, punctual, reliable, purposeful, strong willed, and determined. High C is associated with academic and occupational achievement, although it may lead to annoying fastidiousness, compulsive neatness, or workaholic behavior.

Low C is not necessarily lacking in moral principles, but it is less exacting in applying them, and it is more lackadaisical in working toward goals. There is some evidence indicating that people scoring a low C are more hedonistic. A coach can help a client develop more C by improving the client's process of planning, organizing, and carrying out tasks.

SKILLS ASSESSMENT

It is vital for anyone to fully understand his top interests, skills, talents, strengths, and experiences and to know how and when to use the information.

Understanding My Accomplishments

Spend some time thinking about your career accomplishments and then list three of them below. Don't be modest! This is not the time to be shy about what you have accomplished. First, take a look at this example.

Accomplishment Example: My team and I introduced a major product that we had been testing for about six months. I obtained agreement on the strategic and tactical plan, presented it to management, and won approval for the budget necessary to launch the product.

Now you try it. Remember, these are work accomplishments you enjoyed doing, did well, and found satisfying.

Accomplishment 1:

_____

_____

_____

_____

_____

Accomplishment 2:

_____

_____

_____

_____

Accomplishment 3:

_____

_____

_____

_____

_____

Now ask yourself, "What did I do to make these accomplishments happen?" List the strengths it took to achieve your accomplishments.

Understanding My Strengths

Using the accomplishments example above, the strengths you might list are these:

1. I *planned* the approach.

2. I *communicated* with my team and management.

3. I *marketed* my idea.

4. I *created* a budget.

5. I *sold* the concept.

Other examples of verbs to use in this list are *analyzed, identified, marketed, motivated, negotiated, persuaded, planned, resolved, sold, trained, communicated,* and *wrote.*

Now make your list based on your three accomplishments.

Accomplishment 1: What Did I Do to Make This Happen?	Accomplishment 2: What Did I Do to Make This Happen?	Accomplishment 3: What Did I Do to Make This Happen?
1.	1.	1.
2.	2.	2.
3.	3.	3.
4.	4.	4.
5.	5.	5.

What have you learned about your skills and strengths? How many showed up in all three accomplishments? Use this exercise to catalog and better understand your personal portfolio of skills and strengths and the role they played in your accomplishments. You'll find that these skills, which you used in the work you enjoyed, did well, and found satisfying, will surface again and again in most of your accomplishments.

In addition, think about your core technical skills. These are skills you learned on the job and do well, such as cost accounting, development, finance, mergers, public relations, sales training, and strategic planning.

MY CORE TECHNICAL SKILLS

1.

2.

3.

4.

5.

Now, using the previous exercises, write one or two sentences that you can use to promote yourself when the opportunity arises. Here's an example from a lawyer in a corporate setting:

Self-promotion paragraph: "I am head of the litigation department for my company, and I have negotiated hundreds of lawsuits that saved my company millions of dollars in legal fees. I frequently represent the company by speaking at legal conferences about our experiences with these issues, giving us a reputation as one of the leaders in our industry."

Those two sentences demonstrate experience and skills in law, negotiations, speaking, public relations, and leadership. It is a jam-packed, powerful illustration of how to link your skills with your experiences.

Now it's your turn to compose a sentence or two about yourself. Remember to note an accomplishment and link it to your skills and your technical knowledge:

I am:

_____

_____

_____

_____

TRAINING SEMINARS FOR A BULLY-PROOF WORKPLACE

Practicing the Essentials in Business: Integrity, Etiquette, and Civility

An individual's technical skills and knowledge can contribute only so much to her professional image. Learning integrity, business etiquette, and civility is an important undertaking for anyone looking to make a good impression and a positive impact on her colleagues, clients, managers, and potential employers. Ideal for midlevel professionals looking to advance their careers, this seminar includes examples, self-assessments, and easily applicable tips for introductions, dining habits, business protocol, and physical and emotional presence.

Objectives

- Participants will assess their knowledge of accepted etiquette at work-related functions.

- Participants will learn how to develop and maintain business relationships, project a professional image, and exude confidence.

- Participants will practice speaking and behaving in a manner that is fitting for a bully-proof workplace.

Building Personal Resilience and Courage

Today the old adage "The only constant is change" has never been more accurate. And the pace of change has accelerated. Some of these changes energize and stimulate us; some bring hard times and cause negative stress.

Do you ever wonder why some people come through periods of disappointment or hard times even stronger, whereas others become victims of their circumstances? Much of the answer is rooted in a person's resilience and courage. The good news is that techniques for increasing both personal resilience and courage and the ability to bounce back after hard times can be learned. This seminar will discuss strategies for how to become more resilient and courageous, including self-assessments.

Building Positive Assertive Communication Skills

Communication is the cornerstone of success in all aspects of work. This interactive module includes an overview of the tips and techniques effective communicators use to manage up, down, and across their organizations. Participants will share communication challenges and learn the power of assertive communications. The session will highlight the words, wisdom, self-confidence, and timing assertive communicators employ to enhance their executive presence. Role playing and group discussions will provide participants with a variety of approaches and solutions.

OBJECTIVES

- Participants will assess their current level of assertiveness.

- Participants will learn the different consequences associated with passive, assertive, and aggressive communication styles.

- Participants will be able to identify the language and style appropriate to interactions with their stakeholders.

- Participants will learn a communication model to manage conflict calmly and correctly.

- Participants will come to understand their negotiation style and how that style affects the outcomes they want to achieve.

Developing a Career: Getting in Touch with Your Strengths and Skills

Participants will be led through an interactive session that explores their skills, strengths, and career interests. An individual can take control over his career progression only if he understands his personal portfolio of skills, interests, and motivated abilities. The discussion will include an exercise that is designed to give individuals knowledge and ownership over their career planning and growth.

A gap analysis will determine which experiences and skills each participant needs to acquire to achieve her potential and ideal job. A conversation will be led about how an individual can mesh her identified skills, strengths, and interests with the needs of a civic, community, or nonprofit organization to gain additional experience, contacts, and job satisfaction. In conclusion, participants will be encouraged to take control over their own careers, and they will be given the encouragement and guidelines to do so.

OBJECTIVES

- Understanding the depth and breadth of their predominant strengths and skills and how they affect performance

- Determining which skills and experiences they need to gain to grow in their career

- Dialoguing on career development principles in today's workplace to make the participants aware of their responsibilities in managing their careers effectively

- Identifying the next or ideal job and mapping out a plan to get there

Building Your Personal Brand in a Bully-Proof Workplace

Many emerging leaders are not aware of the importance of the impact their integrity, communication skills, appearance, personal presence, and self-introduction has on others. This half-day program emphasizes participative learning, and it is delivered in a professional, interactive manner with respect, nonjudgmental humor, and content that is accessible and relevant. Participants will develop an awareness of the importance of presenting themselves like professionals, and they will learn how the choices they make can affect productivity.

Topics covered in this session include these:

- The Authentic You: Your Personal Brand

- Impressions People Have of You

- Looking Like a Professional

- Impact and Presence: Getting Your Message Heard Internally and Externally

- That First Impression: You Have Only One Shot

- Your Elevator Speech: Don't Talk About the Weather

Practicing Giving and Receiving Feedback: A Crucial Practice

Giving and receiving feedback is an obligation of all members of an organization, but in most organizations, exploring the best ways to handle feedback is often not given the necessary priority. This session will focus on how one can develop simple techniques to create a learning and open work environment that encourages dialogue and feedback. This session will discuss the importance of regularly seeking feedback and setting developmental goals for oneself and others. Participants will learn communication techniques to support their continued development.

Making Room for Emotional Intelligence at Work

Emotional intelligence (EI) is a key element in building and maintaining strong stakeholder relationships. This module focuses attention on the core skills used by emotionally intelligent people and the importance of emotional intelligence in creating a high-performing, collaborative work environment. Drawing on the work of Daniel Goleman on emotional intelligence, six styles of leadership are discussed and practiced. Each style will emerge naturally in a business simulation, and participants' use of that style will be recorded using an observation methodology. Additionally, each participant will complete an online assessment tool of his or her own emotional intelligence.

OBJECTIVES

- Participants will learn how to use the appropriate style at the appropriate time and to teach others the same.

- Participants will work from their own EQ Map results and develop ways to enhance their skills in their work.

Developing a Confident Presence in Times of Stress

This module focuses on the key characteristics required of high-level executives in the workplace to support and enhance their leadership. The segment provides practical tools and techniques to develop leadership ability regardless of the current level of experience. In this interactive session, participants will learn the elusive qualities that give an executive the impact and presence to have a significant and positive influence on others.

Objectives

- Analysis of the top leadership qualities, such as decisiveness, effective communication skills, and dealing with pressure

- Guiding participants in identifying their strengths and how to apply them in leadership roles

- Analysis of the key characteristics and traits associated with women who are perceived to have dynamic impact and presence

- Suggestions to obtain feedback on one's communication style, leadership abilities, and impact

Practicing the Essential Interpersonal Skills to Enhance Your Gravitas

This seminar gives participants the techniques and tools to master essential skills that will enable them to become an "everyday, everywhere" leader. Participants will learn how to seize the potential in any interaction to lead positively and authentically and be able to share positive ideas and goals while working beyond the status quo. This segment will carry forward on the four voices of leadership and combine the seven learning essentials necessary for positive and progressive leadership.

The seven LEADERS essential skills discussed are these: listening to learn, empathizing with emotions, attending to aspirations, diagnosing and detailing for decision-making, engaging with ethics, responding with respectfulness, and speaking with specificity.

In this segment, participants will also explore the concept of situational leadership and learn the skills necessary to adapt their leadership style to varying circumstances.

OBJECTIVES

- Become a proactive contributor to any effort or team

- Harness the power of interpersonal relationships

- Confront, analyze, and work through any situation

- Create a mentoring, nonthreatening environment for colleagues

Understanding Political Savvy to Optimize Your Influence

Through an interactive discussion, participants will analyze their ability to get things done and develop a deeper understanding of the organizational and cultural dynamics of the organization. Participants will learn new strategies to be even more effective in their work as they explore the underlying political structure of the organization.

The further one advances in an organization, the more important it is to progress beyond just having good ideas to garnering the support of others to move an idea forward. Truly excellent influencing skills require a healthy balance of interpersonal communication and assertiveness techniques with political savvy. This interactive event is designed to demonstrate a variety of influencing techniques that men and women can utilize to work with others.

OBJECTIVES

- Learning to map stakeholders on an issue they support and how to develop a strategy for building critical mass to move forward

- Discovering important influencing tactics and how they can be utilized to positively affect their role in their organization

- Using a self-assessment test to identify which influencing tactics can work strategically with subordinates, peers, or supervisors

- Learning how influencing tactics can begin to build and expand credibility

- Developing action steps to effectively increase influence throughout the organization

Managing Conflict, Confrontation, and Difficult Conversations

As a leader, your position of power often demands having difficult conversations, conveying tough messages, and resolving conflicts within your team or with your subordinates. Through this interactive session, participants will learn skills, techniques, and strategies for managing difficult, important conversations and addressing conflict in a professional manner. The session incorporates role playing, video clips, small group activities, and skills practice to develop a mastery of interpersonal problem solving.

This module focuses on gaining a mastery of interpersonal problem-solving skills and dealing with difficult conversations, particularly those aspects of motivation, emotion, and ability that are relevant to complex conflict situations. The topic of how a manager addresses ability, motivation, emotion, and other complex problems in the workplace that can lead to conflict is also addressed.

Participants learn the following skills:

- Using positive reinforcement

- Communicating situations with accuracy

- Diagnosing emotion, motivation, and complexity within conflict

- Asking, listening, and hearing other people's ideas

- Paraphrasing the commentary of others to understand them better

- Probing for details, discernment, and decision-making

- Determining who does what by when

Strategic Networking That Builds Social Capital

Organizational leaders utilize networking to expand their sphere of influence and to accomplish business goals. This module will provide participants with the opportunity to examine the role of networking in achieving their personal, professional, and organizational goals. Participants will evaluate their personal and professional networks and learn how to leverage their networks to achieve personal and professional goals. Strategies and tactics will be discussed on how to build and enhance their key stakeholder relationships, which are critical in achieving optimal business and professional results.

OBJECTIVES

- Identifying the strategic importance of and the value of building a dynamic professional network

- Identifying key stakeholders and developing strategies for enhancing these relationships

- Assessing one's own network and how it will contribute to career success

- Developing skills and strategies to improve one's network and especially key stakeholder relationships

- Practicing networking skills and strategies useful from introductions to follow-up communications

Team Effectiveness: Developing a Group into a Team

A good leader needs to foster a sense of teamwork, leverage differences, and facilitate the effective interaction and contribution of others. Participants will learn to facilitate a group process that ensures that each member's voice and vote is heard with equal measure—irrespective of rank, seniority, and credentials—and results in team development and value-added productivity.

This optimizes the input for successful envisioning of the future, decision-making, and planning. Using the *nominal group technique* (NGT) with a video simulation, participants will learn the technique for team decision-making and the optimal involvement of others. The NGT brings together a group of people through all the stages of team development. This interactive session demonstrates the power of collective focus on problems at work and shows the process toward solutions. Listening without judgment coupled with constructive feedback is a powerful two-step approach to developing teamwork and thinking holistically about organizational performance improvement.

Workplace Bullying: How to Create Inclusiveness at Work

Bullying in the workplace is a critical issue that is growing in scope within the corporate world. Bullying is the intentional mistreatment of others that can cause physical and/or psychological harm. It is present in all industries and at all levels, and it can have a negative impact on the bottom line. Bullying can be overt or subtle in its delivery. Examples include criticizing someone in front of his coworkers or giving a risky assignment that jeopardizes the target's job. In this presentation, participants will learn the macro- and micro-inequities of behaviors that are considered mistreatment and how to prevent becoming a practitioner or recipient of bullying. Participants also will discover how to create a positive, inclusive workplace for themselves and their teams.

NOTES

PROLOGUE

1. http://es.pn/Mjtkz4.
2. http://read.bi/29mIrFV.

CHAPTER 1

1. Charlotte Rayner and Cary Cooper, "Workplace Bullying: Myth or Reality—Can We Afford to Ignore It?" *Leadership & Organization Development Journal,* vol. 18, no. 4, 1997, pp. 211–214; and Charlotte Rayner and Helge Hoel, *Workplace Bullying: What Do We Know, Who Is to Blame and What Can We Do?* Taylor & Francis, New York, 2001.
2. Jill Brooke, *The Need to Say No: How to Be Bullish Without Being Bulldozed,* Hatherleigh Press, New York, 2013.
3. According to the Workplace Bullying Institute (WBI) 2012 *Impact of Workplace Bullying on Individuals' Health* survey report, bullying drove 71 percent of targets to seek treatment from a physician; an alarming 29 percent contemplated suicide (*2014 WBI U.S. Workplace Bullying Survey,* February 2014, Gary Namie, PhD, research director, with assistance from Daniel Christensen and David Phillips).
4. National Institute for Occupational Safety and Health (NIOSH) in 2006 reported that 24.5 percent of the companies surveyed said that some degree of bullying had occurred there during the preceding year and 55.2 percent involved the employee as the "victim," www.cdc.gov/niosh/topics/stress/ (http://www.cdc.gov/niosh/topics/stress).
5. According to the Healthy Workplace Campaign (HWC), fortified with the WBI's Healthy Workplace Bill, bullying is four times more prevalent than illegal discrimination, yet it's still legal in the United States.
6. See more at www.workplacebullying.org/tag/shrm.

7. WBI 2012 *Impact of Workplace Bullying on Individuals' Health.*

8. Andrea Adams and Neil Crawford, *Bullying at Work*, Virago and Little Brown Book Group, London, England,1992.

9. Christine Porath and Christine Pearson, "The Price of Incivility," *Harvard Business Review* (HBR), January-February 2013.

10. Accountemps Survey, *Managers Spend Nearly a Full Day Each Week Dealing with Staff Conflicts*, Menlo Park, CA, March 15, 2011.

11. The American Institute of Stress (AIS) is a nonprofit organization that provides information on stress reduction and stress in the workplace.

12. Workplace bullying is on the rise, yet despite the prevalence of bullying and its damaging impact, organizational responses are spotty, at best, according to Terri Howard, vice president of corporate preparedness for the Crisis Prevention Institute (CPI), the world's leader in crisis preparedness and intervention.

13. www.knowbull.com.

14. http://www.workplacebullying.org/individuals/solutions/costs/.

15. Ralph Estes, *Tyranny of the Bottom Line: Why Corporations Make Good People Do Bad Things*, Berrett-Koehler, Oakland, CA, 1995.

16. Frederick Winslow Taylor, *The Principles of Scientific Management*, Harper & Brothers, New York, 1911; and Frederick Winslow Taylor, *Scientific Management*, Harper & Brothers, New York, 1947.

17. U.S. Department of Labor, Occupational Safety and Health Administration, *Guidelines for Preventing Workplace Violence for Healthcare and Social Service Workers*, OSHA Publication 3148-04R, 2015, p.2.

18. One-half (51 percent) of organizations reported that there had been incidents of bullying in their workplace. The three most common outcomes of bullying incidents that organizations reported were decreased morale (68 percent), increased stress and/or depression levels (48 percent), and decreased trust among coworkers (45 percent). This is Part 1 of a two-part series of SHRM survey findings on workplace bullying and violence. See www.shrm.org/research/surveyfindings/articles/pages/workplacebullying .aspx#sthash.s2qcUSks.dpuf.

19. Christine Pearson and Christine Porath, *The Cost of Bad Behavior: How Incivility Is Damaging Your Business and What to Do About It*, Penguin/ Portfolio, New York and London, 2009.

20. Gary Namie and Ruth Namie, *The Bully-Free Workplace: Stop Jerks, Weasels & Snakes from Killing Your Organization*, Wiley, Hoboken, NJ, 2011; and Gary Namie and Ruth Namie, *The Bully at Work: What You Can Do to Stop the Hurt and Reclaim Your Dignity on the Job*, 2d ed., Sourcebooks, Naperville, IL, 2009.

CHAPTER 2

1. Barbara Pachter, *The Power of Positive Confrontation*, Marlowe & Company, New York, 2000.
2. Christine Pearson and Christine Porath, *The Cost of Bad Behavior: How Incivility Is Damaging Your Business and What to Do About It*, Penguin/Portfolio, New York and London, 2009.
3. Karl A. Menninger, *The Human Mind Revisited: Essays in Honor of Karl A. Menninger*, edited by Sydney Smith, International Universities Press, Topeka, KS, 1978; and Kansas Historical Society, "Karl Menninger," http://www.kshs.org/kansapedia/karl-menninger/17218. Accessed December 3, 2014: http://www.searchquotes.com/search/Karl_Menninger/.
4. J. C. Flanagan, "The Critical Incident Technique," *Psychological Bulletin*, vol. 51, no. 4, July 1954, pp. 327–357.

CHAPTER 3

1. P. J. Dean, *A Critical Incident Study Investigating the Perceived Effective and Ineffective Leadership Behaviors of Iowa Community College Presidents*, ERIC Clearinghouse, ERIC number ED3I8, 504, 1986; and P. J. Dean, *A Critical Incident Study Investigating the Perceived Effective and Ineffective Leadership Behaviors of Iowa College Presidents*, PhD dissertation, University of Iowa, Iowa City, 1986.

CHAPTER 4

1. P. J. Dean, *A Critical Incident Study Investigating the Perceived Effective and Ineffective Leadership Behaviors of Iowa Community College Presidents*, ERIC Clearinghouse, ERIC number ED3I8, 504, 1986; and P. J. Dean, *A Critical Incident Study Investigating the Perceived Effective and Ineffective Leadership Behaviors of Iowa College Presidents*, PhD dissertation, University of Iowa, Iowa City, 1986.

CHAPTER 5

1. P. J. Dean, *A Critical Incident Study Investigating the Perceived Effective and Ineffective Leadership Behaviors of Iowa Community College Presidents*, ERIC Clearinghouse, ERIC number ED3I8, 504, 1986; and P. J. Dean, *A Critical Incident Study Investigating the Perceived Effective and Ineffective Leadership Behaviors of Iowa College Presidents*, PhD dissertation, University of Iowa, Iowa City, 1986.

CHAPTER 6

1. P. J. Dean, *A Critical Incident Study Investigating the Perceived Effective and Ineffective Leadership Behaviors of Iowa Community College Presidents*, ERIC Clearinghouse, ERIC number ED318, 504, 1986; and P. J. Dean, *A Critical Incident Study Investigating the Perceived Effective and Ineffective Leadership Behaviors of Iowa College Presidents*, PhD dissertation, University of Iowa, Iowa City, 1986.

CHAPTER 7

1. www.CoolNSmart.com/bullying_quotes/page/2/.
2. Molly Crockett, "No Fair! My Serotonin Level Is Low," Scientific American, 60-Second Mind, podcast, June 9, 2008, http://www.scientificamerican .com/podcast/episode/68fc98f1-e48a-251d-8f65277181db9a4e/.
3. Margaret R. Kohut, *The Complete Guide to Understanding, Controlling and Stopping Bullies and Bullying at Work: A Guide for Managers, Supervisors and Employees*, Atlanta Publishing, 2008.

CHAPTER 8

1. Thomas Gilbert, *Human Competence: Engineering Worthy Performance*, International Society for Performance Improvement, Washington, DC, and HRD Press, Amherst, MA, 1996.
2. P. J. Dean, with M. D. Shepard and Monica L. Warner, *The Coachable Leader: What Future Executives Need to Know Today*, iUniverse, Bloomington, IN, 2011.
3. John P. Kotter, *Accelerate: Building Strategic Agility for a Fast-Moving World*, Harvard Business School Publishing, Boston, 2014.
4. P. J. Dean, with M. D. Shepard and Monica L. Warner, *The Coachable Leader: What Future Executives Need to Know Today*, iUniverse, Bloomington, IN, 2011.
5. Kathleen Patel, *The Bullying Epidemic: The Guide to Arm You for the Fight*, Smashwords.com Books, 2011, http://www.goodreads.com/book/show/ 13318539-the-bullying-epidemic-the-guide-to-arm-you-for-the-fight.
6. P. J. Dean, *Leadership for Everyone: How to Apply the Seven Essential Skills to Become a Great Motivator, Influencer, and Leader*, McGraw-Hill, New York, 2006.
7. Edgar H. Schein, *Humble Inquiry: The Gentle Art of Asking Instead of Telling*, Berrett-Koehler, San Francisco, 2013.

8. P. J. Dean, with M. D. Shepard and Monica L. Warner, *The Coachable Leader. What Future Executives Need to Know Today*, iUniverse, Bloomington, IN, 2011.

9. http://employeeengagement.com/wp-content/uploads/2013/06/Gallup -2013-State-of-the-American-Workplace-Report.pdf; and http://www .gallupstudentpoll.com/174020/2013-gallup-student-poll-overall-report .aspx.

10. Jacob Morgan, *The Future of Work: Attract New Talent, Build Better Leaders, and Create a Competitive Organization*, Wiley, Hoboken, NJ, 2014.

CHAPTER 9

1. Robert Greenleaf, *Servant Leadership: A Journey into the Nature of Legitimate Power and Greatness*, 25th ed., Paulist Press, Mahwah, NJ, 2002.

2. Carl Rogers, "A Theory of Therapy, Personality, and Interpersonal Relationships, as Developed in the Client-Centered Framework," in S. Koch (ed.), *Psychology: A Study of Science*, McGraw-Hill, New York, 1959. See also Carl Rogers, *A Way of Being*, Houghton Mifflin, Boston, 1980.

3. P. J. Dean, "Setting Standards for Right and Wrong," *Financial Times*, October 15, 2001; P. J. Dean, "Making Codes of Ethics Real," *Journal of Business Ethics*, vol. 11, 1992, pp. 285–290; P. J. Dean, "Customizing Codes of Ethics to Set Professional Standards," *Performance Improvement Journal*, vol. 33, no. 2, ISPI Publications, 1994, pp. 36–45; and P. J. Dean, "A Qualitative Method of Assessment and Analysis for Changing Organizational Culture," *Performance Improvement Journal*, vol. 37, no. 2, ISPI Publications, 1997, pp. 14–23.

BIBLIOGRAPHY AND ADDITIONAL RESOURCES

Albrecht, K., and R. Zemke. *Service America! Doing Business in the New Economy*. Grand Central Publishing, New York, 1990.

Amen, D. G. *Change Your Brain Change Your Life: The Breakthrough Program for Conquering Anxiety, Depression, Obsessiveness, Anger and Impulsiveness*. Three Rivers Press, New York, 1998.

Anderson, F. H. Learning in Discussions: A Résumé of the Authoritarian-Democratic Studies." *Harvard Educational Review*, vol. 229, 1959, pp. 201–215.

Argyris, C. "How Normal Science Methodology Makes Leadership Research Less Additive and Less Applicable." In J. G. Hunt and L. L. Larsen (eds.), *Crosscurrents in Leadership*, Southern Illinois University Press, Carbondale, 1979, pp. 47–63.

———. *Reasoning, Learning, and Action: Individual and Organizational*. Jossey-Bass/Wiley, Hoboken, NJ, 1982.

———. *Knowledge for Action: A Guide to Overcoming Barriers to Organizational Change*. Jossey-Bass/Wiley, Hoboken, NJ, 1993.

———. *Reasoning, Learning and Action*. Harper Business, New York, 1997.

Argyris, C., and D. A. Schon. *Organizational Learning: A Theory of Action Perspective*. Addison-Wesley, Reading, MA, 1980.

Austin, L. *What's Holding You Back? 8 Critical Choices for Women's Success*. Perseus, New York, 2001.

Axelrod, D. "Getting Everyone Involved: How One Organization Involved Its Employees, Supervisors, and Managers in Redesigning the Organization." *Journal of Applied Behavioral Science*, vol. 28, no. 4, 1992, pp. 499–509.

Babcock, L. *Women Don't Ask: Negotiation and the Gender Divide*. Princeton University Press, Princeton, NJ, 2003.

Baker, W. *Achieving Success Through Social Capital*. Jossey-Bass/Wiley, New York, 2000.

Bales, R. F. "Task Roles and Social Roles in Problem-Solving Groups." In E. E. Maccoby, T. M. Newcomb, and E. L. Wartley (eds.), *Reading in Social Psychology*, 3rd ed., Henry Holt, Baltimore, 1958, pp. 437–447.

Banathy, B., and P. Jenlink. *Dialogue as a Means of Collective Communication*. Springer/Academic/Plenum, Berlin, Germany, 2005.

Barnett, R. *Same Difference: How the Gender Myths Are Hurting Our Relationships, Our Children, and Our Jobs*. Perseus, New York, 2004.

Barsh, J., S. Cranston, and R. Craske. "Centered Leadership: How Talented Women Thrive." *McKinsey Quarterly*, September 2008.

Baumann, Peter, and Michael W. Taft. *Ego: The Fall of the Twin Towers and the Rise of an Enlightened Humanity*. NE PRESS, San Francisco, 2011.

Bazerman, Max H., and Ann E. Tenbrunsel. *Blind Spots: Why We Fail to Do What's Right and What to Do about It*. Princeton University Press, Princeton, NJ, 2011.

Bechtle, Mike. *People Can't Drive You Crazy If You Don't Give Them the Keys*. Revell, Baker Publishing Group, Grand Rapids, MI, 2012.

Behary, Wendy T. *Disarming the Narcissist: Surviving and Thriving with the Self-Absorbed*. New Harbinger, Oakland, CA, 2013.

Bell, E. L., and S. Nkomo. *Our Separate Ways: Black and White Women and the Struggle for Professional Identity*. Harvard Business School Publishing, Boston, 2003.

Bennis, W. *On Becoming a Leader*. Perseus Press, New York, 1994.

Bennis, W., and B. Nanus. *Leaders: The Strategies for Taking Charge*. HarperCollins, New York, 1985.

Bennis, W. G., K. D. Benne, and R. Chin. *The Planning for Change.* Holt, Rinehart and Winston, New York, 1985.

Bensimon, E. M., and A. Neumann. *Redesigning Collegiate Leadership: Teams and Teamwork in Higher Education.* Johns Hopkins University Press, Baltimore, 1993.

Benton, D. A. *Lions Don't Need to Roar: Using the Leadership Power of Personal Presence to Stand Out, Fit in, and Move Ahead.* Grand Central Publishing, New York, 1993.

Berkowitz, L. "Sharing Leadership in Small, Decision-Making Groups." *Journal of Abnormal and Social Psychology,* vol. 48, 1953, pp. 231–238.

Bjorseth, L. *Breakthrough Networking: Building Relationships That Last.* Duoforce Enterprises, Lisle, IL, 1996.

Block, P. *Stewardship.* Berrett-Koehler, Oakland, CA, 1996.

Bohm, D. *On Dialogue.* David Bohm Seminars, Routledge, Abingdon-on-Thames, United Kingdom, 2004.

Bohm, D., and M. Edwards. *Changing Consciousness, Exploring the Hidden Source of the Social, Political, and Environmental Crises Facing Our World.* Pegasus Books, New York, 1992.

Bolton, Sharon C. *Dimensions of Dignity at Work.* Butterworth-Heinemann/Elsevier, Amsterdam, Netherlands, 2007.

Bowditch, J. L., and A. F. Buono. *A Primer on Organizational Behavior.* Wiley, Hoboken, NJ, 1997.

Bowman, E., and B. Kogut. *Redesigning the Firm.* Oxford University Press, New York, 1995.

Brandon, R., and M. Seldman. *Survival of the Savvy: High-Integrity Political Tactics for Career and Company Success.* Free Press, New York, 2004.

Branson, D. M. *No Seat at the Table: How Corporate Governance Keeps Women out of the Boardroom.* New York University Press, New York, 2008.

Brewer, J. H., M. J. Ainsworth, and G. E. Wynne. *Power Management.* Prentice Hall, Upper Saddle River, NJ, 1984.

Brinkman, R., and R. Kirschner. *Dealing with People You Can't Stand: How to Bring Out the Best in People at Their Worst.* McGraw-Hill, New York, 2002.

Brizendine, L. *The Female Brain*. Morgan Road Books, New York, 2007.

———. *The Male Brain*. Three Rivers Press, New York, 2011.

Brouwer, P. "The Power to See Ourselves." *Harvard Business Review*, November 1964.

Bunker, B. B., and B. T. Alban (eds.). *Large Group Interventions*, Special Issue. *Journal of Applied Behavioral Science*, vol. 28, no. 4, 1992.

Burgoon, J. K. "Nonverbal Signals." In M. L. Knapp and G. R. Miller (eds.), *Handbook of Interpersonal Communication*. SAGE, Thousand Oaks, CA, 1985, pp. 83–85.

Burns, J. M. *Leadership*. Harper, New York, 1978.

Cain, Susan. *Quiet: The Power of Introverts in a World That Can't Stop Talking*. Crown, New York, 2012.

Chamine, Shirzad. *Positive Intelligence: Why Only 20% of Teams and Individuals Achieve Their True Potential and How You Can Achieve Yours*. Greenleaf, Austin, TX, 2012.

Charan, R. *What the CEO Wants You to Know: How Your Company Really Works*. Crown, New York, 2001.

Ciampa, D., and M. Watkins. *Right from the Start: Taking Charge in a New Leadership Role*. Harvard Business School Press, Boston, 1999.

Collins, Jim. "Level 5 Leadership: The Triumph of Humility and Fierce Resolve." *Harvard Business Review*, February 2001.

———. *Good to Great: Why Some Companies Make the Leap . . . and Others Don't*. Harper Business/HarperCollins, New York, 2001.

Coutu, D. L. "How Resilience Works." *Harvard Business Review*, May 2002.

Cramer, Kathryn D. *Lead Positive: What Highly Effective Leaders See, Say, and Do*. Jossey-Bass/Wiley, Hoboken, NJ, 2014.

Crane, D., and P. Moreton. *Salomon and the Treasury Securities Auction*. Harvard Business School Case Number 9-292-114, 1992.

Cuddy, Amy. *Presence: Bringing Your Boldest Self to Your Biggest Challenge*. Little, Brown, New York, 2015.

Cummings, T. G., and C. G. Worley. *Organization Development and Change*. West Publishing, Eagan, MN, 1993.

D'Alessandro, D. F. *Career Warfare: 10 Rules for Building a Successful Brand and Fighting to Keep It*. McGraw-Hill, New York, 2004.

Daft, R., and R. Lengel. *Unlocking the Subtle Forces That Change People and Organizations.* Berrett-Koehler, Oakland, CA, 1998.

Dean, Peter J. *The Effects of TM Technique on Concept Formation, Autonomic Stability, and EEF Coherence.* Brain Science Research, MS master thesis, MIU, Fairfield, IA, 1980.

————. *Guidelines for the Implementation of Change by a Change Team.* Unpublished manuscript. University of Iowa, Iowa City, 1983.

————. *A Critical Incident Study Investigating the Perceived Effective and Ineffective Leadership Behaviors of Iowa Community College Presidents.* ERIC Clearinghouse, #ED318, 504, 1986.

————. "Making Codes of Ethics Real." *Journal of Business Ethics,* vol. 11, 1992, pp. 285–290.

————. "Customizing Codes of Ethics to Set Professional Standards." *Performance Improvement Journal,* vol. 33, no. 2, ISPI Publications, 1994, pp. 36–45.

————. "Examining the Practice of Human Performance Technology." *Performance Improvement Quarterly,* vol. 8, no. 2, 1995, pp. 68–94.

————. "A Qualitative Method of Assessment and Analysis for Changing Organizational Culture." *Performance Improvement Journal,* vol. 37, no. 2, ISPI Publications, 1997, pp. 14–23.

————. *Performance Engineering at Work.* International Board of Standards for Training, Performance and Instruction, IBSTPI Publications and International Society for Performance Improvement, ISPI Publications, 1999.

————. "Setting Standards for Right and Wrong." *Financial Times,* October 15, 2001.

————. *Leadership for Everyone: How to Apply the Seven Essential Skills to Become a Great Motivator, Influencer, and Leader.* McGraw-Hill, New York, 2006.

Dean, Peter J., with M. D. Shepard and Monica L. Warner. *The Coachable Leader: What Future Executives Need to Know Today.* iUniverse, Bloomington, IN, 2011.

Dean, Peter J., and D. E. Ripley (eds.). *Performance Improvement Interventions: Methods for Organizational Learning. Instructional Design and Training, Volumes 2 and 3.* International Society of Performance Improvement, Silver Spring, MD, 1998.

Dean, Peter J., and D. E. Ripley. *Performance Improvement Pathfinders: Models for Organizational Learning Systems.* International Society for Performance Improvement, Silver Spring, MD, 1997.

Dean, Peter J., J. K. Brooke, and L. B. Shields. "Examining the Skills of Speaking for Shared Meaning." *Performance Improvement Journal,* vol. 35, no. 6, 1996, pp. 4–9.

Dean, Peter J., M. R. Dean, and E. Guman. "Identifying a Range of Performance Improvement Solutions: High Yield Training to Systems Redesign." *Performance Improvement Quarterly,* vol. 5, no. 4, 1992, pp. 175–185.

Dean, Peter J., S. Blevins, and P. J. Snodgrass. "Performance Analysis: An HRD Tool That Drives Change in Organizations." In J. J. Phillips and E. F. Holton III (eds.), *Action: Leading Organizational Change,* American Society for Training and Development, Alexandria, VA, 1997.

De Geus, A. "The Living Company: Habits for Survival in a Turbulent Business Environment." *Harvard Business Review,* March-April 1997.

Delbecq, A. L., and A. H. Van de Ven. "A Group Process Model for Problem Identification and Problem Planning." *Journal of Applied Behavioral Science,* vol. 7, 1971, pp. 466–492.

DeLuca, J. *Political Savvy: Systematic Approaches to Leadership Behind-the-Scenes.* Evergreen Business Group (EBG) Publications, Berwyn, PA, 1999.

DePree, Max. *Leadership Is an Art.* Broadway Business, New York, 2004.

Donaldson, T., and T. Dunfee. "Toward a Unified Conception of Business Ethics: Integrative Social Contract Theory." *Academy of Management Review,* vol. 19, no. 2, 1994, pp. 252–284.

Drath, W. H., and C. J. Palus. *Making Common Sense: Leadership as Meaning-Making in a Community of Practice.* Center for Creative Leadership (CCL), Greensboro, NC, 1994.

Drucker, P. "What Communication Means," Chapter 38. *Management: Tasks, Responsibilities, Practice.* Harper & Row, New York, 1974.

———. "Management and the World's Work." *Harvard Business Review*, September 1988.

———. *The Ecological Vision: Reflections on the American Condition*. Transaction Publishers, Piscataway, NJ, 1993.

Duffy, Maureen, and Len Sperry. *Overcoming Mobbing: A Recovery Guide for Workplace Aggression and Bullying*. Oxford University Press, New York, 2014.

Duhigg, Charles. *The Power of Habit: Why We Do What We Do in Life and Business*. Random House, New York, 2014.

Emery, F. E. *Systems Thinking*. Penguin, London, United Kingdom, 1978.

———. "Participative Design: Effective, Flexible, and Successful, Now!" *Journal for Quality and Participation*, vol. 18, no. 1, 1995, pp. 6–9.

Emery, F. E., and E. L. Trist. "Socio-Technical Systems." In C. W. Churchman et al. (eds.), *Management Sciences, Models, and Techniques*. Pergamon, Oxford, United Kingdom, 1960.

Emery, F. E., and E. L. Trist. *Toward a Social Ecology*. Plenum/Springer, Berlin, Germany, 1973.

Emery, M. (ed.). *Participative Design for Participative Democracy*. Center for Continuing Education, Australian National University, Canberra, 1993.

Emery, M., and R. E. Purser. *The Search Conference: Theory and Practice*. Jossey-Bass/Wiley, Hoboken, NJ, 1996.

Erikson, E. "Identity and the Life Cycle," *Psychological Issues*, vol. 1, no. 1, International Universities Press, Madison, CT.

Estes, Ralph. *Tyranny of the Bottom Line: Why Corporations Make Good People Do Bad Things*. Berrett-Koehler, Oakland, CA, 1996.

Evans, G. *Play Like a Man, Win Like a Woman: What Men Know About Success That Women Need to Learn*. Broadway Books, New York, 2000.

Feiner, M. *The Feiner Points of Leadership: The 50 Basic Laws That Will Make People Want to Perform Better for You*. McGraw-Hill, New York, 2004.

Field, Tim. *Bully in Sight: How to Predict, Resist, Challenge, and Combat Workplace Bullying*. Success Unlimited, 1996, bullyonline.org.

Fifty Lessons (author). *Managing Your Career (Lessons Learned)*. Harvard Business School Publishing, Boston, 2007.

Finkelstein, S. *Why Smart Executives Fail*. Penguin, New York, 2003.

Fisher, D. *Professional Networking for Dummies*. Wiley, Hoboken, NJ, 2001.

Fisher, D., and S. Vilas. *Power Networking: 59 Secrets for Personal and Professional Success*. Bard Press, Austin, TX, 2000.

Fisher, H. *The First Sex: The Natural Talents of Women and How They Are Changing the World*. Ballantine/Random House, New York, 2000.

Flanagan, J. C. "The Critical Incident Technique." *Psychological Bulletin*, vol. 51, no. 4, July 1954, pp. 327–357.

Fleishmann, E. A., E. Harris, and H. Burtt. *Leadership and Supervision in Industry: An Evaluation of a Supervisory Training Program*. Ohio State Bureau of Educational Research, 1955.

Frankel, L. *Nice Girls Don't Get the Corner Office: 101 Unconscious Mistakes Women Make That Sabotage Their Careers*. Warner Business, Anderson, IN, 2004.

Frankfurt, Harry G. *On Truth*. Alfred A. Knopf, New York, 2009.

———. *The Importance of What We Care About*, Cambridge University Press, New York, 2009.

Freeman, R. Edward. *Business Ethics: The State of the Art*. Oxford University Press, New York, 1991.

Freud, S. *The Standard Edition of the Complete Psychological Works of Sigmund Freud*. Hogarth Press and Institute of Psycho-Analysis, London, 1963; and 16, III: *Introductory Lectures on Psycho-Analysis*, J. Strachey (ed.). Originally published 1917.

Fromm, E. *Escape from Freedom*. Holt, Rinehart and Winston, New York, 1941.

Galbraith, Jay R. *Organization Design*. Addison-Wesley, Reading, MA, 1977.

———. *Designing Organizations*, Jossey-Bass/Wiley, Hoboken, NJ, 1995.

Galbraith, Jay R., and E. D. Lawler. *Organizing for the Future*. Jossey-Bass/Wiley, Hoboken, NJ, 1993.

Gardner, J. *On Leadership*. Free Press, New York, 1993.

Garvin, D. A. "Building a Learning Organization." *Harvard Business Review*, July-August 1993, pp. 78–91.

Gelles, David. *Mindful Work: How Meditation Is Changing Business from the Inside Out*. An Eamon Dolan Book, Houghton Mifflin Harcourt, Boston, 2015.

George, B., and W. Bennis. *Authentic Leadership: Rediscovering the Secrets to Creating Lasting Value*. Jossey-Bass/Wiley, Hoboken, NJ, 2004.

Gepson, J., M. J. Martinko, and J. Belina. "Nominal Group Techniques." *Training and Development Journal*, September 1981, pp. 78–83.

Geroy, G. D., and P. C. Wright. "Evaluation Research: A Pragmatic, Program-Focused Research Strategy for Decision Makers." *Performance Improvement Quarterly*, vol. 1, no. 3, 1988, pp. 17–26.

Ghiselli, E. "Managerial Talent." *American Psychology*, vol. 16, 1963, pp. 109–113.

Ghoshal, S., and C. A. Bartlett. *The Individualized Corporation*. Harper Business, New York, 1997.

Giblin, Les. *How to Have Confidence and Power in Dealing with People*. Prentice Hall, Upper Saddle River, NJ, 1956.

Gilbert, T. F. *Human Competence: Engineering Worthy Performance*. McGraw-Hill, New York, 1978.

———. "A Question of Performance—Part I: The PROBE Model." *Training and Development Journal*, September 1982, pp. 21–30.

———. "A Question of Performance—Part II: Applying the PROBE Model." *Training and Development Journal*, October 1982, pp. 85–89.

———. Personal interview. 1991.

———. *Human Competence: Engineering Worthy Performance*. International Society for Performance Improvement, Silver Spring, MD, 1996.

Gilley, J. W., P. J. Dean, and L. Bierema. *Philosophy and Practice of Organizational Learning, Performance, and Change*. Perseus, New York, 2001.

Giovagnoli, M., and J. Carter-Miller. *Networlding: Building Relationships and Opportunities for Success*. Wiley, Hoboken, NJ, 2000.

Gladwell, Malcolm. *The Tipping Point: How Little Things Can Make a Big Difference*. Little, Brown, New York, 2000.

Godin, Seth. *Wisdom, Inc.: 26 Business Virtues That Turn Ordinary People into Extraordinary Leaders*. Harper Business/HarperCollins, New York, 1995.

Goffman, Irving. *The Presentation of Self in Everyday Life*. Anchor Books/Doubleday, New York, 1959.

Goleman, Daniel. *Emotional Intelligence*. Bantam, New York, 1997.

———. *Focus: The Hidden Driver of Excellence*. HarperCollins, New York, 2013.

Govindarajan, V., and C. Trimble. *Ten Rules for Strategic Innovators: From Idea to Execution*. Harvard Business School Press, Boston, 2005.

Graham, P. (ed.). *Mary Parker Follett: The Prophet of Management*. Harvard Business School Press, Boston, 1995.

Grant, Adam. *Give and Take: Why Helping Others Drives Our Success*. Penguin, New York, 2013.

Greenleaf, Robert. *Servant Leadership: A Journey into the Nature of Legitimate Power and Greatness*. Paulist Press, Mahwah, NJ, 1977.

———. *Servant Leadership: A Journey into the Nature of Legitimate Power and Greatness*, 25th ed. Paulist Press, Mahwah, NJ, 2002.

Groysberg, B. "How Star Women Build Portable Skills." *Harvard Business Review*, February 2008.

Hamilton, N. Gregory. *Self and Others: Object Relations Theory in Practice*. Jason Aronson, Northvale, NJ, 1990.

Hammer, M., and J. Champy. *Reengineering the Corporation: A Manifesto for Business Revolution*. Harper Business, New York, 1993.

Hankin, H. *The New Workforce: Five Sweeping Trends That Will Shape Your Company's Future*. AMACOM, New York, 2004.

Hanson, G. A., R. T. Hanson, and T. D. Stoddard. *Say It Right: Guide to Effective Oral Business Presentations*. Irwin/McGraw-Hill, New York, 1995.

Hare, A. P. "Small Group Discussion with Participatory and Supervisory Leadership." *Journal of Abnormal Social Psychology*, vol. 48, 1953, pp. 273–275.

Hare, Robert D. *Without Conscience: The Disturbing World of the Psychopaths Among Us.* Guilford Press, New York, 1999.

Harvard Business Review. HBR's 10 Must Reads on Managing Yourself. HBR Press, Boston, 2010.

Haudan, Jim. *The Art of Engagement: Bridging the Gap Between People and Possibilities.* McGraw-Hill, New York, 2008.

Hayward, Mathew. *Ego Check: Why Executives Hubris Is Wrecking Companies and Careers and How to Avoid the Trap.* Kaplan Publishing, Chicago, 2007.

Heenan, D., and W. Bennis. *Co-Leaders: The Power of Great Partnerships.* Wiley, Hoboken, NJ, 1999.

Heifetz, R. *Leadership Without Easy Answers,* Harvard University Press, Cambridge, MA, 1998.

Hersey, P., and K. H. Blanchard. *Management of Organizational Behavior: Utilizing Human Resources.* Prentice Hall, Upper Saddle River, NJ, 1982.

Hersey, P., K. H. Blanchard, and R. K. Hambleton. "Contracting for Leadership Style: A Process and Instrumentation for Building Effective Work Relationships." In W. W. Burke (ed.), *The Cutting Edge: Current Theory and Practice in Organizational Development,* University Associates, San Francisco, 1978, pp. 214–237.

Hewlett, Sylvia Ann. "Executive Women and the Myth of Having It All." *Harvard Business Review,* April 2002.

———. *Executive Presence: The Missing Link Between Merit and Success.* HarperCollins, New York, 2014.

Hillman, J. *Kinds of Power: A Guide to Its Intelligent Uses.* Doubleday, New York, 1995.

Holmes, J. *Gendered Talk at Work: Constructing Gender Identity Through Workplace Discourse.* Blackwell, Malden, MA, 2006.

Horney, K. *Neurosis and Human Growth: The Struggle Toward Self-Realization.* Norton, New York, 1950.

House, R. "Path-Goal Theory of Leadership: Lessons, Legacy and Reformulated Theory." *Leadership Quarterly,* vol. 7, no. 3, 1974, pp. 323–352.

Hunter, J. C. *The World's Most Powerful Leadership Principles*. Random House, New York, 2005.

Hupp, T. R. Personal correspondence. President, Organizations by Design, Warrenville, IL, 1998.

Isaacs, W. *Dialogue and the Art of Thinking Together*. Doubleday, New York, 1999.

Jacobi, J. *The Psychology of C. G. Jung*. Yale University Press, New Haven, CT, 1973.

Jankovich, J. L., and E. A. LeMay. *The Best Guide to Effective Presentations: A Step-by-Step Approach*. College Customs Series. McGraw-Hill, New York, 1997.

Jaworski, J. *Synchronicity*. Berrett-Koehler, Oakland, CA, 1997.

Jennings, E. E. "The Anatomy of Leadership." *Management of Personnel Quarterly*, vol. 1, 1961, pp. 2–9.

Johnson, G. *Research Methodologies for Economists*. Macmillan, London, 1986.

Jung, C. G. *Man and His Symbols*. Doubleday, New York, 1964.

Kantor, R. M. *Confidence: How Winning Streaks & Losing Streaks Begin & End*. Crown Business, New York, 2004.

Katz, D., and R. L. Kahn. *The Social Psychology of Organizations*. Wiley, Hoboken, NJ, 1966.

Katzenbach, J., and D. Smith. *The Wisdom of Teams: Creating the High-Performance Organization*. Harper Paperbacks, New York, 1993.

Katzenbach, J. R., F. Beckett, and C. Gagnon. *Real Change Leaders: How You Can Create Growth and High Performance at Your Company*. Crown, New York, 1997.

Kay, Katty, and Claire Shipman. *The Confidence Code: The Science and Art of Self-Assurance—What Women Should Know*. Harper Business/HarperCollins, New York, 2014.

Kellerman, B. *Bad Leadership: What It Is, How It Happens, Why It Matters*. Harvard Business School Press, Boston, 2004.

Kelley, Robert E. *How to Be a Star at Work: Nine Breakthrough Strategies You Need to Succeed*. Three Rivers Press, New York, 1998.

Keltner, Dacher. *The Power Paradox: How We Gain and Lose Influence.* Penguin, New York, 2016.

Kenigel, Robert. *The One Best Way: Frederick Winslow Taylor and the Enigma of Efficiency.* Viking/Penguin, New York, 1997.

Kepcher, C., and S. Fenichell. *Carolyn 101: Business Lessons from The Apprentice's Straight Shooter.* Fireside, New York, 2004.

Kirschner, Rick, and Rick Brinkman. *Dealing with People You Can't Stand: How to Bring Out the Best in People at Their Worst.* McGraw-Hill, New York, 2012.

Klaus, P. *Brag: The Art of Tooting Your Own Horn Without Blowing It.* Warner Press, Anderson, IN, 2003.

Kleiner, A. *Who Really Matters: The Core Group Theory of Power, Privilege, and Success.* Doubleday, New York, 2003.

Klepper, M. M. *I'd Rather Die Than Give a Speech: A Comprehensive Guide for Public Speaking.* Irwin/McGraw-Hill, New York, 1994.

Kluger, Jeffrey. *The Narcissist Next Door: Understanding the Monster in Your Family, in Your Office, in Your Bed— in Your World.* Riverhead Books/Penguin, New York, 2014.

Kofodimos, J. R. *Balancing Act: How Managers Can Integrate Successful Careers and Fulfilling Personal Lives.* Jossey-Bass/Wiley, Hoboken, NJ, 1993.

Kohut, Margaret R. *The Complete Guide to Understanding, Controlling and Stopping Bullies and Bullying at Work: A Guide for Managers, Supervisors, and Employees.* Atlanta Publishing Group, Atlanta, 2008.

Kolb, D. M., J. Williams, and C. Frohlinger. *Her Place at the Table: A Woman's Guide to Negotiating Five Key Challenges to Leadership Success.* Wiley, Hoboken, NJ, 2004.

Kolb, D., and J. Williams. *The Shadow Negotiation: How Women Can Master the Hidden Agendas That Determine Bargaining Success.* Simon & Schuster, New York, 2000.

Kouzes, J. M., and B. Z. Posner. *The Leadership Challenge: How to Keep Getting Extraordinary Things Done in Organizations.* Jossey-Bass/Wiley, Hoboken, NJ, 1995.

Kouzes, J. M., and B. Z. Posner. *Credibility: How Leaders Gain and Lose It, Why People Demand It.* Jossey-Bass/Wiley, Hoboken, NJ, 1995.

Kreamer, Anne. *It's Always Personal: Emotion in the New Workplace.* Random House, New York, 2011.

Kuhn, T. S. *The Structure of Scientific Revolutions.* University of Chicago Press, Chicago, 1970.

Larimore, W., and B. Larimore. *His Brain, Her Brain.* Zondervan, Grand Rapids, MI, 2008.

Lawrence, P. R., and J. W. Lorsch. *Developing Organizations: Diagnosis and Action.* Addison-Wesley, Reading, MA, 1969.

Leavitt, H. J. "Unhuman Organizations." *Harvard Business Review,* vol. 40, no. 4, 1962, pp. 90–98.

Lencioni, Patrick. *The Five Dysfunctions of a Team: A Leadership Fable.* Jossey-Bass/Wiley, Hoboken, NJ, 2002.

Lewin, K. "Behavior and Development as a Function of the Total Situation." In C. Carmichael (ed.), *Manual of Child Psychology,* Wiley, Hoboken, NJ, 1946.

———. "Frontiers in Group Dynamics, Part 1: Concept, Method and Reality in Social Science: Social Equilibria and Social Change." *Human Relations,* vol. 1, 1947, pp. 5–41.

———. "Frontiers in Group Dynamics, Part 2: Channels of Group Life: Social Planning and Action Research." *Human Relations.* vol. 1, 1947, pp. 143–153.

———. *Resolving Social Conflicts.* Harper & Row, New York, 1948.

———. *Field Theory in Social Science.* HarperCollins, New York, 1951.

Lichtenberg, R. *Pitch Like a Girl: How a Woman Can Be Herself and Still Succeed.* Rodale Press, New York, 2005.

Likert, R. *New Patterns of Management.* McGraw-Hill, New York, 1961.

———. *The Human Organization.* McGraw-Hill, New York, 1967.

———. "Future Before You Plan." In R. A. Ritvo and A. G. Sargent (eds.), *The NTL Managers' Handbook,* NTL Institute, Arlington, VA, 1983.

Lippitt, R., and C. Jung. "Utilization of Scientific Knowledge for Change in Education." *Concepts for Social Change.* vol. 5, no. 1, 1966, pp. 25–29.

Loden, M. *Implementing Diversity: Best Practices for Making Diversity Work in Your Organization*. McGraw-Hill, New York, 1995.

Maltby, Lewis. *Can They Do That? Retaking Our Fundamental Rights in the Workplace*. Portfolio/Penguin, New York, 2009.

Marquardt, M. J., and T. Carter. "Action Learning at George Washington University." *Performance Improvement Quarterly*, vol. 11, no. 2, pp. 59–71, 1998.

Maslow, A. H. "A Theory of Human Motivation." *Psychological Review*, vol. 50, 1943, pp. 370–396.

Maxwell, J. C. *The 21 Indispensable Qualities of a Leader: Becoming the Person Others Will Want to Follow*. Thomas Nelson, Nashville, TN, 1999.

Mayo, E. *The Social Problems of an Industrial Civilization*. Harvard Business School, Boston, 1945.

McGregor, D. *The Human Side of Enterprise*. McGraw-Hill, New York, 1960.

McLagan, P., and N. Christo. *The Age of Participation*. Berrett-Koehler, Oakland, CA, 1995.

Medalia, N. Z. "Authoritarianism, Leader Acceptance, and Group Cohesion." *Journal of Abnormal and Social Psychology*, vol. 51, 1955, pp. 207–213.

Mehrabian, A. "Communicating Without Words." *Psychology Today*, vol. 2, no. 9, 1968, pp. 52–55.

———. *Silent Messages: Implicit Communication of Emotions and Attitudes*, 2d ed. Wadsworth/Cengage, Boston, 1981.

Metrix Global LLC, *Executive Briefing: Case Study on the Return on Investment of Executive Coaching*. Merrill Anderson, PhD, 2001.

Miles, R. E., and C. C. Snow. *Organizational Strategy, Structure and Process*. McGraw-Hill, New York, 1978.

Miller, L. E., and J. Miller. *A Woman's Guide to Successful Negotiating: How to Convince, Collaborate, and Create Your Way to Agreement*. McGraw-Hill, New York, 2002.

Mlodinow, Leonard. *Subliminal: How Your Unconscious Mind Rules Your Behavior*. Vintage Books/Random House, New York, 2012.

Mohrman, S. A., and T. G. Cummings. *Self-Designing Organizations: Learning How to Create High Performance*. Addison-Wesley, Boston, 1989.

Monarth, Harrison. *Executive Presence: The Art of Commanding Respect Like a CEO*. McGraw-Hill, New York, 2010.

Morrison, T., C. A. Wayne, and G. A. Borden. *Kiss, Bow, or Shake Hands*. Adams Media Corporation, Avon, MA, 1994.

Nadler, D. A., and M. L. Tushman. *Competing by Design: The Power of Organizational Architecture*. Oxford University Press, New York, 1997.

Nadler, D. A., M. S. Gerstein, and R. B. Shaw. *Organizational Architecture: Designs for Changing Organizations*. Jossey-Bass/Wiley, Hoboken, NJ, 1992.

Namie, Gary, and Ruth Namie. *The Bully at Work: What You Can Do to Stop and Reclaim Your Dignity on the Job*. Sourcebooks, Workplace Bullying Institute, 2009, www.workplacebullying.org.

Namie, Gary, and Ruth Namie. *The Bully-Free Workplace: Stop Jerks, Weasels, and Snakes from Killing Your Organization*. Wiley, Hoboken, NJ, 2011.

Nanus, B., and W. Bennis. *Strategies for Taking Charge*. Harper Business, New York, 1997.

Neff, T. J., and J. Citrin. *Lessons from the Top*. Doubleday, New York, 1999.

Neffinger, John, and Matthew Kohut. *Compelling People: The Hidden Qualities That Make Us Influential*. Hudson Street Press/Penguin, New York, 2013.

Nye, Joseph S. *The Future of Power*. Public Affairs/Perseus, New York, 2011.

Oshry, B. *Seeing Systems: Unlocking the Mysteries of Organizational Life*. Berrett-Koehler, Oakland, CA, 1995.

———. *Leading Systems: Lessons from the Power Lab*. Berrett-Koehler, Oakland, CA, 1999.

Pachter, B. *The Power of Positive Confrontation: The Skills You Need to Know to Handle Conflict at Work, Home, and in Life*. Marlowe/Avalon, New York, 2001.

————. *When the Little Things Count . . . And They Always Count: 601 Essential Things That Everyone in Business Needs to Know*. Marlowe/Avalon, New York, 2001.

Pachter, B., and M. Brody. *The Complete Business Etiquette Handbook*. Prentice Hall, Upper Saddle River, NJ, 1994.

Paine, L., and M. Santoro. *Sears Auto Centers (A)*. Harvard Business School Case Number 394-009, July 1993.

Paine, L. S. "Managing for Organizational Integrity." *Harvard Business Review*, March-April 1994.

Parks, S. D. *Leadership Can Be Taught: A Bold Approach for a Complex World*. Harvard Business School Press, Boston, 2005.

Patterson, K., J. Grenny, D. Maxfield, and R. McMillan. *Influencer: The Power to Change Anything*. McGraw-Hill, New York, 2007.

Patterson, Kerry, and Joseph Grenny. *Crucial Conversations: Tools for Talking When Stakes Are High*. McGraw-Hill, New York, 2011.

Pearson, Christine, and Christine Porath. *The Cost of Bad Behavior: How Incivility Is Damaging Your Business*. Portfolio/Penguin, New York, 2009.

Pegues, Deborah Smith. *Confronting Without Offending: Positive and Practical Steps to Resolving Conflict*. Harvest House, Eugene, OR, 2009.

Pfeffer, Jeffrey. *Leadership BS: Fixing Workplace and Careers One Truth at a Time*. Harper Business, HarperCollins, New York, 2015.

Piaget, J. *Jean Piaget: The Man and His Ideas*. Norton, New York, 1973.

Pink, D. H. *A Whole New Mind: Why Right-Brainers Will Rule the World*. Riverhead, New York, 2006.

Pinkley, R. L., and G. B. Northcraft. *Get Paid What You're Worth: The Expert Negotiators' Guide to Salary and Compensation*. St. Martin's Press/Macmillan, New York, 2003.

Prentice, W. "Understanding Leadership." *Harvard Business Review*, vol. 39, 1953, pp. 143–151.

Reardon, K. *The Secret Handshake: Mastering the Politics of the Business Inner Circle*. Doubleday, New York, 2002.

Reddin, W. J. "The 3-D Management Style Theory." *Training and Development Journal*, vol. 21, 1967, pp. 8–17.

———. *Managerial Effectiveness*. McGraw-Hill, New York, 1970.

Reivich, K., and A. Shatte. *The Resilience Factor: 7 Keys to Finding Your Inner Strength and Overcoming Life's Hurdles*. Broadway, New York, 2003.

Reynolds, Simon. *Why People Fail: The 16 Obstacles to Success and How You Can Overcome Them*. Jossey-Bass/Wiley, Hoboken, NJ, 2012.

Robey, D., and C. A. Sales. *Designing Organizations*. Irwin/McGraw-Hill, New York, 1994.

Roby, T. B. "The Executive Function in Small Groups." In L. Petrullo and B. M. Bass (eds.), *Leadership and Interpersonal Behavior*, Holt, Rinehart and Winston, New York, 1961.

Rogers, C. A. *A Way of Being*. Houghton Mifflin, Boston, 1980.

Rogers, C. R. "A Theory of Therapy, Personality, and Interpersonal Relationships, as Developed in the Client-Centered Framework." In S. Koch (ed.), *Psychology: A Study of Science*. McGraw-Hill, New York, 1959.

Ross, Howard J. *Everyday Bias: Identifying and Navigating Unconscious Judgments in Our Daily Lives*. Rowman & Littlefield, Lanham, MD, 2014.

Rost, J. C. *Leadership for the Twenty-First Century*. Praeger/Greenwood, Santa Barbara, CA, 1991.

Ruderman, M. N., and P. J. Ohlott. *Standing at the Crossroads: Next Steps for High Achieving Women*. Jossey-Bass/Wiley, Hoboken, NJ, 2002.

Rummler, G. A. "Managing the Organization as a System." *Training*, vol. 34, no. 2, 1997, pp. 68–74.

Rummler, G. A., and A. P. Brache. *Improving Performance: How to Manage the White Space on the Organization Chart*. Jossey-Bass/Wiley, Hoboken, NJ, 1990.

Runion, Meryl, and Wendy Mack. *Perfect Phrases for Leadership Development: Hundreds of Ready-to-Use Phrases for Guiding Employees to Reach the Next Level*. McGraw-Hill, New York, 2011.

Russo, J. E., and P. J. Schoemaker. *Decision Traps: Ten Barriers to Brilliant Decision-Making and How to Overcome Them.* Simon & Schuster, New York, 1990.

Ryan, R. *Soaring on Your Strengths: Discover, Use, and Brand Your Best Self for Career Success.* Penguin, New York, 2005.

Sachs, A. *Girls Get Even: Advice Guides Say That Women Don't Have to Be Macho in the Workplace.* Time.com Inside Business, 2006.

Schein, E. *Organizational Culture and Leadership.* Jossey-Bass/Wiley, Hoboken, NJ, 1992.

Schwartz, Barry, and Kenneth Sharpe. *Practical Wisdom: The Right Way to Do the Right Thing.* Riverhead/Penguin, New York, 2010.

Seay, T. A., and M. K. Altefruse. "Verbal and Nonverbal Behavior in Judgments of Facilitative Conditions." *Journal of Counseling Psychology*, vol. 26, 1979, pp. 108–119.

Segal, Jeanne. *The Language of Emotional Intelligence: The Five Essential Tools for Building Powerful and Effective Relationships.* McGraw-Hill, New York, 2008.

Segal, M. *Points of Influence: A Guide to Using Personality Theory.* Jossey-Bass/Wiley, Hoboken, NJ, 1997.

Senge, Peter M. *The Fifth Discipline: The Art and Practice of the Learning Organization.* Currency/Random House, New York, 1994.

Senge, P. M., A. Kleiner, C. Roberts, R. B. Ross, and B. J. Smith. *The Fifth Discipline Field Book: Strategies and Tools for Building a Learning Organization.* Doubleday, New York, 1994.

Shell, G. R., and M. Moussa. *The Art of Woo: Using Strategic Persuasion to Sell Your Ideas.* Portfolio, Middlesex, United Kingdom, October 2007.

Shepard, M. D. *Stop Whining & Start Winning: 8 Surefire Ways for Women to Thrive in Business.* Penguin, New York, 2005.

Shepard, M. D., J. K. Stimmler, and P. J. Dean. *Breaking into the Boys' Club: 8 Ways for Women to Get Ahead in Business.* Rowman & Littlefield, Lanham, MD, 2009.

Shepherd, Margaret. *The Art of Civilized Conversation: A Guide to Expressing Yourself with Style and Grace.* Broadway, New York, 2005.

Shriberg, A., D. Shriberg, and R. Kumari. *Practicing Leadership: Principles and Practices*. Wiley, Hoboken, NJ, 2005.

Skinner, B. F. *Beyond Freedom and Dignity*. Hackett, Indianapolis, IN, 1971.

Stevens, R. A. "The Hospital as a Social Institution." *Hospital and Health Services Administration*, vol. 36, Summer 1991, pp. 163–173.

———. *Handbook of Leadership: A Survey of the Literature*. Free Press, New York, 1974.

Stogdill, R. M., and A. E. Coons (eds.). *Leader Behavior: Its Description and Measurement*, Monograph 83. Bureau of Business Research, Ohio State University, Columbus, 1957.

Stutz, Phil, and Barry Michels. *The Tools: Transform Your Problems into Courage, Confidence, and Creativity*. Spiegel & Gray/Random House, New York, 2012.

Tanenbaum, L. *Catfight: Women and Competition*. Seven Stories Press, 2002.

Tannen, D. *You Just Don't Understand: Women and Men in Conversation*. William Morrow/HarperCollins, New York, 1990.

Tannenbaum, R., and W. H. Schmidt. "How to Choose a Leadership Pattern." *Harvard Business Review*, vol. 25, 1957, pp. 95–101.

Taylor, F. W. *The Principles of Scientific Management*. Harper & Brothers, New York, 1911.

———. *Scientific Management*. Harper & Brothers, New York, 1947.

Tepper, D. T., and R. F. Hasse. "Verbal and Nonverbal Communication of Facilitative Conditions." *Journal of Counseling Psychology*, vol. 25, 1978, pp. 35–44.

Tett, Gilliam. *The Silo Effect: The Peril of Expertise and the Promise of Breaking Down Barriers*. Simon & Schuster, New York, 2015.

Tichy, N., and E. B. Cohen. *The Leadership Engine: How Winning Companies Build Leaders at Every Level*. Harper Business, New York, 1997.

Toler, Stan. *Outstanding Leadership*. Harvest House, Eugene, OR, 2016.

Toogood, G. N. *The Articulate Executive: Learn to Look, Act, and Sound Like a Leader*. McGraw-Hill, New York, 1996.

Torrance, E. P. "Methods of Conducting Critiques of Group Problem-Solving Performance." *Journal of Applied Psychology*, vol. 37, 1953, pp. 394–398.

Trist, E. *The Evolution of Socio-Technical Systems: A Conceptual Framework and an Action Research Program*, Occasional Paper No. 2. Ontario Quality of Working Life Centre, 1981.

Tuckman, B. W. *Conducting Education Research*, 2d ed. Harcourt, Brace & Jovanovich, New York, 1978.

Tushman, M. L., and C. O'Reilly. "Ambidextrous Organizations: Managing Evolutionary and Revolutionary Change." *California Management Review*, vol. 38, no. 4, 1996, pp. 8–30.

Tushman, M. L., C. O'Reilly, and D. A. Nadler. *The Management of Organizations: Strategies, Tactics, Analyses*. Harper & Row. New York, 1989.

Ulrich, Dave, Norm Smallwood, and Kate Sweetman. *The Leadership Code: Five Rules to Lead By*. Harvard Business School Press, Boston, 2008.

Utterback, J. *Mastering the Dynamics of Innovation*. Harvard Business School Press, Boston, 1994.

von Bertalanffy, L. *General Systems Theory*. Braziller, New York, 1950.

———. *Problems of Life*. Wiley, Hoboken, NJ, 1952.

Vrato, E. *The Counselors: Conversations with 18 Courageous Women Who Have Changed the World*. Running Press, Philadelphia, 2003.

Vroom, V. H., and P. Yetton. *Leadership and Decision-Making*. University of Pittsburgh Press, 1973.

Walton, Clarence C. *The Moral Manager*. Ballinger, Cambridge, MA, 1988.

Watkins, K. E., and V. J. Marsick. *Sculpting the Learning Organization: Lessons in the Art and Science of Systemic Change*. Jossey-Bass/Wiley, Hoboken, NJ, 1993.

Watkins, M. *The First 90 Days: Critical Success Strategies for New Leaders at All Levels*. Harvard Business School Publishing, Boston, 2003.

Weinberg, G. M. *An Introduction to General Systems Thinking*. Wiley, Hoboken, NJ, 1975.

Weinholtz, D. *A Study of Instructional Leadership During Medical Attending Rounds*. PhD dissertation. University of North Carolina, 1981.

Weisbord, M. R. *Productive Workplaces: Organizing and Managing for Dignity, Meaning, and Community*. Jossey-Bass/Wiley, Hoboken, NJ, 1987.

———. *Discovering Common Ground*. Berrett-Koehler, Oakland, CA, 1992.

Weisbord, M. R., and S. Janoff. *Future Search*. Berrett-Koehler, Oakland, CA, 1995.

Welzler, Scott. *Living with the Passive-Aggressive Man: Coping with the Personality Syndrome of Hidden Aggression—from the Bedroom to the Boardroom*. Fireside/Simon & Schuster, New York, 1992.

Wheatley, M. J. *Leadership and the New Science*. Berrett-Koehler, Oakland, CA, 1992.

———. *A Simpler Way*. Berrett-Koehler, Oakland, CA, 1997.

Whitney, C. *Nine and Counting: The Women of the Senate*. HarperCollins, New York, 2000.

Williams, D. *Real Leadership: Helping People and Organizations Face Their Toughest Challenges*. Berrett-Koehler, Oakland, CA, 2005.

Wilson, K. K., and S. Salee. "Use Your Head: Insights on the Differences Between Women's and Men's Brains and What These Differences Mean." *Women Lawyers Journal*, vol. 90, no. 4, Summer 2005, pp. 26–28.

Yankelovich, D. *The Magic of Dialogue*. Simon & Shuster, New York, 1991.

Zahn, G. L. "Cognitive Integration of Verbal and Vocal Information in Spoken Sentences." *Journal of Experimental Social Psychology*, vol. 9, 1973, pp. 320–334.

Zander, R. S., and B. Zander. *The Art of Possibility*. Harvard Business School Press, Boston, 1973, 2000.

Zelazny, G. *Say It with Presentations: How to Design and Deliver Successful Business Presentations*. McGraw-Hill, New York, 2000.

Zichy, S., and B. Kellen. *Women and the Leadership Q: Revealing the Four Paths to Influence and Power*. McGraw-Hill, New York, 2000.

Zigarmi, D., K. Blanchard, M. O'Connor, and C. Edeburn. *The Leader Within: Learning Enough About Yourself to Lead Others.* FT Press/Pearson, Upper Saddle River, NJ, 2004.

Zmud, R. W., and C. P. McLaughlin. "That's Not My Job: Managing Secondary Tasks Effectively." *Sloan Management Review*, vol. 30, no. 3, 1989.

INDEX

ABOUT THE AUTHORS

Peter J. Dean, MS, PhD, and **Molly D. Shepard,** MS, MSM, are joint partners in The Leaders Edge/Leaders By Design, a leadership development and executive coaching firm dedicated to helping boards, C-suite executives, and high-potential leaders. Their programs are focused on enhancing the leadership skills of women and men, including their ability to embrace, understand, and leverage the complexities inherent in a diverse workforce.

They have consulted and coached for major companies, such as ARAMARK, AstraZeneca, Bristol-Myers Squibb, Campbell Soup Company, Comcast, Chubb, DuPont, GlaxoSmithKline, Independence Blue Cross, Children's Hospital of Philadelphia, Johnson & Johnson, KPMG, Lincoln Financial, Novartis, Microsoft, MetLife, Shire, Nasdaq, Pfizer, Exelon, Teva Pharmaceuticals, University of Pennsylvania Health System, Wawa, and Wilmington Trust.

Peter has been on the faculty at the Wharton School and the Fels Center of Government at the University of Pennsylvania, Penn State University, Fordham University, the University of Iowa, the University of Tennessee, and the American College, teaching courses in leadership, change management, ethics, and communications. He was honored with teaching awards at Penn State University, the Wharton School, and the University of Tennessee. He designed two master's degree programs for Penn State University in instructional systems and management. He codesigned the physician executive MBA program at the University of Tennessee.

Peter was editor of *Performance Improvement Quarterly* and board director of the International Board of Standards for Training, Performance and Instruction. Two of the ten books he has authored include, *Leadership for Everyone: How to Apply the Seven Essential Skills to Become a Great Motivator, Influencer, and Leader* and *The Coachable Leader: What Future Executives Need to Know Today*.

Peter holds an MS in organizational dynamics from the University of Pennsylvania and a PhD in education from the University of Iowa. He has lived and consulted in Europe and Asia for eight years.

Molly has more than 25 years of experience in career counseling, leadership development, executive coaching, and executive search. Through her leadership as chairperson, president, and cofounder of Manchester Inc., one of the world's largest career development consulting firms, she helped develop the highest standards for excellence in program design and delivery. Under her guidance, Manchester became one of the nation's top human resources consulting firms, helping thousands of people a year transition into new jobs and reach their potential as leaders. It was subsequently acquired by AccuStaff Inc. Before that, Molly was regional vice president of Hay Career Consultants, a division of the Hay Group, and previously vice president of Diversified Search Inc., a Philadelphia-based executive search firm.

Molly has served on numerous nonprofit and for-profit boards, and she is chair emeritus of the United Way of Southeastern Pennsylvania and WHYY Inc. and president emeritus of the Pennsylvania Women's Forum. Molly is a member of the board of directors of the Greater Philadelphia Chamber of Commerce, the National Multiple Sclerosis Society–Greater Delaware Valley Chapter, and WHYY Inc.

Molly received the Brava! Achievement Award, given to a top regional female CEO by *SmartCEO* magazine, the Trailblazer Award from *Philadelphia Magazine*, the *Philadelphia Business Journal*'s Women of Distinction Award, the Beta Gamma Sigma Award from the LeBow College of Business at Drexel University, the Woman One Award from Drexel University College of Medicine, and the Greater Philadelphia Chamber of Commerce Paradigm Award as the outstanding woman business leader of the year.

Molly is the coauthor of *Breaking into the Boys' Club* and *Stop Whining and Start Winning* (Penguin, 2005).

Molly holds a BA from Wheaton College, an MS in psychological services and counseling from the University of Pennsylvania, an MSM in leadership from American College, and an honorary doctorate of humanities from West Chester University.

Molly and Peter are married to each other and are the parents of four children. They live in Philadelphia, Pennsylvania.

For more information or to book a presentation, please e-mail peterdean5000@aol.com.